D0425926

THE
SCOTTSBORO
BOYS

THE
SCOTTSBORO
BOYS

·JAMES HASKINS·

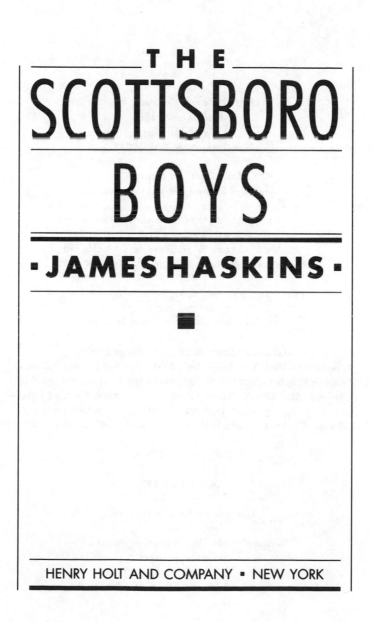

HENRY HOLT AND COMPANY · NEW YORK

Henry Holt and Company, Inc.
Publishers since 1866
115 West 18th Street
New York, New York 10011

Henry Holt is a registered
trademark of Henry Holt and Company, Inc.

Published in Canada by Fitzhenry & Whiteside Ltd.,
195 Allstate Parkway, Markham, Ontario L3R 4T8.

Library of Congress Cataloging-in-Publication Data
Haskins, James.
The Scottsboro Boys / by James Haskins.
p.   cm.
Includes bibliographical references and index.
1. Scottsboro Trial, Scottsboro, Ala., 1931—Juvenile literature. 2. Trials
(Rape)—Alabama—Scottsboro—Juvenile literature. [1. Scottsboro Trial,
Scottsboro, Ala., 1931. 2. Trials (Rape) 3. Afro-Americans—Civil rights—
History] I. Title.
KF224.S34H37 1994   345.761'9502532—dc20 [347.6195052532]   93-42331

ISBN 0-8050-2206-6

First Edition—1994

Designed by Victoria Hartman

Printed in the United States of America
on acid-free paper.

1 3 5 7 9 10 8 6 4 2

TO CATHY

I am grateful to Anne Jordan
and Kathy Benson for their help.

CONTENTS

INTRODUCTION 3

1. HARD TIMES A-COMING 5

2. PAINT ROCK, ALABAMA 13

3. "A FAIR AND LAWFUL TRIAL" 23

4. "LET THOSE PORE BOYS GET FREE" 33

5. *POWELL V. ALABAMA* 43

6. ANOTHER "FAIR TRIAL" 52

7. CALLAHAN'S COURT 63

8. *NORRIS V. ALABAMA* 72

9. BACK TO DECATUR 79

10. FINAL TRIALS AND TRIBULATIONS 88

11. THE AFTERMATH 96

AFTERWORD 104

NOTES 107

BIBLIOGRAPHY 112

INDEX 113

THE
SCOTTSBORO
BOYS

INTRODUCTION

On March 25, 1931, nine black men and boys were pulled from a slow freight train in Paint Rock, Alabama, because of a report that they had been brawling with a group of white men. The nine had been roped together and loaded onto a truck to be taken to nearby Scottsboro when two white women who had also been on the train approached the Paint Rock deputy sheriff and said the blacks had sexually assaulted them. Thus began one of the most famous cases of injustice in American history.

Charged with rape, what was then the most serious crime that could be committed in the South, the Scottsboro Boys, as they came to be known, never had a chance in the Alabama justice system. Although they insisted they had not even known that the women were on the train, they were quickly tried and convicted and condemned to death.

Fortunately, outsiders stepped in to help the Scottsboro Boys. Unfortunately, these outsiders were Communists. Many Americans, especially in the South, saw communism as a threat to the American way of life and regarded Communist help for the Scottsboro Boys as further evidence that the nine should die, or at least spend the remainder of their lives in prison. Four of the Scottsboro Boys spent six years in prison, the other five longer. The last Scottsboro Boy finally released himself by escaping from an Alabama prison farm in 1948.

For a great many Americans who were born since the 1960s, the idea that nine young black men could spend so many years in prison for a crime they did not commit is difficult to accept. But the 1930s were different times, in more ways than just attitudes about race.

They were times when the nation was in the midst of the Great Depression, when millions of people were out of work and without homes. They were times when it was easy to blame others who looked different or believed in different ideas. In Germany, Adolf Hitler was gaining power with his message that Jews were to blame for his country's economic woes and with his call for racial purity. In this country, a similar message could be heard against blacks, Jews, and Communists, but those who proclaimed it never achieved Hitler's power. The American systems of government and justice prevailed, but in the case of the Scottsboro Boys, just barely. This is how it happened.

1
HARD TIMES
A-COMING

Poverty knew no section, no occupation, no age. The Negro middle class as well as the lower class was decimated by the Great Depression. Competition for even the most menial positions destroyed the concept of "Negro jobs"—employment so demanding or repulsive that many whites refused to do it.

—Gilbert Osofsky, *The Burden of Race*[1]

The stock market crash of October 29, 1929, financially destroyed the lives of thousands of people. On that day, however, few predicted the consequences the crash would have; few foresaw that it would herald the most severe and longest depression the United States had ever faced. The immediate results, of course, were sensationally trumpeted across the country by radio and newspapers. Pictures were printed of frenzied investors and stockbrokers trying to salvage what little they could on the floor of the New York Stock Exchange. Stories were widespread of those who had lost everything in the crash plunging to their deaths from their office windows.

Even in the immediate aftermath of the crash, the general public assumed there would be a quick recovery. The crazy, free-spending Roaring Twenties had not prepared them for a world in which both money and jobs were, for all purposes, nonexistent. As the decade turned, recovery seemed to grow more distant, however, and bewilderment and disillusionment rapidly replaced the former optimism. No group felt the Great Depression more or suffered as much as the black population of the United States. Black men and women had been occupying the bottom rung of the economic and social ladder even before disaster struck. With the Great Depression, many were left with little more than the shirts on their backs.

The freedom and opportunities most black people had hoped for after the Civil War had been quickly stifled by the enactment of countless segregation laws across the country, and especially in the South, separating blacks from whites. These laws were often called Jim Crow laws, after a popular minstrel character—Daddy "Jim Crow" Rice—a white man in blackface who played a comical Negro character. Not only were restaurants, rest-room facilities, schools, and streetcars segregated in many towns and cities, but certain jobs were denied to black men and women. Poll taxes and literacy tests restricted their voting. The first three decades of the twentieth century had been marked by a hardening of anti-black sentiment.

The Great Depression only served to intensify racial disparities. Desperate for any job, white men and women seized jobs formerly held by blacks. Open hostility by whites raged against those blacks still working in the face of white unemployment. To make way for poor white farmers in the South, for example, black sharecroppers and tenant farmers and their families were forced off lands they had tilled since the end of the Civil War.

The National Association for the Advancement of Colored People (NAACP) registered protests over what was being done to blacks, but politically weak as it was at that time, there was little it could accomplish against the formidable beast of racism, and southern racism in particular. Black leaders spoke against racism. The black intellectual W. E. B. Du Bois felt that blacks must set up separate communities and establish their own economy. This isolationist position by one of the most influential black leaders of the day dismayed the NAACP and all of those who were fighting for equality and integration.

As the Great Depression ground on, more and more people fell victim to it. Out of work, often homeless, blacks and whites took to the roads in search of jobs.

The economy had been further weakened by a collapse of the agricultural industry in the Midwest. Once rich and fertile, the land had supported many in the Great Plains states such as Oklahoma and Kansas. But wasteful farming techniques had eroded the soil, turning that region into a "dust bowl." With nothing to hold it down, the soil formed great choking clouds of dust scouring the barren land, blowing away the livelihood of thousands of small farmers.

The "Okies" of the dust bowl, impoverished migrant farm workers who were often from Oklahoma, joined the thousands already on the roads seeking jobs, roaming from place to place. So many were there, in fact, that California set up border patrols along its state lines to turn away families that had less than $50 in their pockets.

While some took to the roads in dilapidated cars, others, black and white, male and female, hopped trains. These migrants who rode trains came to be called "hoboes." They rode from town to town seeking any job they could find lasting from a day to several weeks, begging handouts and food along the way. "Hobo jungles" grew up alongside railroad tracks in small and large towns. Railroad guards often threw them off the trains on which they hitchhiked, but many guards also looked the other way. With the times the way they were, the guards knew that they could just as easily be the ones crouched in the shadows of that boxcar, riding to another town, the next hope for a job or a living. One female hobo spoke for many when she said, "The country's in an uproar now—it's in bad shape. . . . Do you reckon I'd be out on the highway if I had it good at home?"

One group, however, saw the Great Depression and,

in particular, the plight of the black men and women as an opportunity: The American Communist Party. Suddenly, it seemed, all that they had preached was coming true; it was up to them to exploit the times.

During the 1920s, communism had failed to attract any great numbers of either black or white Americans. Those members of black communities who were impelled to join often found themselves on the fringe both within and outside the party. In New York, for example, Harlem Communists found that party memberships isolated them from the rest of the community. Despite the Communists' cry for equality for all workers regardless of race, many blacks felt that such a movement was a white idea; after all, most of its leaders were white. Blacks could see no benefit from joining the Communist Party. Across the United States, blacks were represented in the Communist Party ranks in far smaller proportions than whites.

With the advent of the Great Depression, more and more people of all races began flocking to the Communist Party. Many were driven by anger and desperation. Homeless and out of a job, workers rationalized that their problems were the result of the abuse of authority by the bosses. Marxist philosophy, upon which communism is based, held that "a diminishing number of capitalists appropriate the benefits of improved industrial methods, while the labouring class are left in increasing dependency and misery."[2] That was why they were jobless; the bosses lived off them, then threw them away. The Communist philosophy of "from each according to his ability; to each according to his need," and the idea of equality of all workers appealed mightily to the victims of the Great Depression. Their need was great indeed. Here was an organization that seemed to recognize their plight and promised to do something about it.

Although the Communist Party in America had advocated racial equality since its inception, the depression was viewed by its leaders as a golden opportunity to reinforce this idea. In 1930, *The Communist* published "The Communist International Resolution on the Negro Question in U.S.," which outlined the opportunities available for enlisting black members and for emancipating them from their capitalistic "overseers" in the United States and around the world. One of the main goals expressed in this document was "to fight for the full rights of the oppressed Negroes and for their right to self-determination and against all forms of chauvinism, especially among the workers of the oppressing nationality."

American Communists felt that the depression was a signal that American capitalism was on its last legs. What was needed was a complete social and economic revolution, and communism, they felt, was the answer. Spurred by the depression, members of the Communist Party began actively recruiting members of all races, and blacks in particular strenuously pursued the ideas of racial equality the Communists espoused.

Despite their lofty intentions, American Communists found it difficult to infiltrate deeply into black communities. In times of hardship, most black men and women turned first to family and neighborhood and then to their churches for aid and solace. Blacks were suspicious of the arguments made by the Communists. White Communists, on the other hand, were often uncomfortable and unenthusiastic about pursuing their ideals in black neighborhoods and communities. Slowly, however, black membership in the party grew. The Communist Party not only seemed to advocate equality and freedom from oppression but also to offer power in leadership and in life to a powerless minority, and to offer help to the jobless.

In 1930, for example, New York City Communists devised a plan for dealing with evictions for nonpayment of rent, a problem faced by many during the depression. The party had previously organized the Harlem Unemployment Council to deal with joblessness. That council now undertook to send interracial defense squads to return the furniture of evicted tenants to their apartments. While not always successful in stopping evictions, the squads did represent action— *something* was being done. In the minds of many blacks at the time, the Communist Party was a force to be utilized when other groups failed. It appeared to be there to help, even in seemingly hopeless situations.

For the purpose of aiding those who seemed unfairly accused of crimes they did not commit, the International Labor Defense (ILD) had been organized by the Communist Party and, in mid-December of 1929, had made the struggle for black rights its primary focus. The ILD not only provided free legal counsel to black defendants, it also organized meetings to protest lynching, police brutality, and racial discrimination.

The call to action by ILD leaders, and their strident rhetoric, appealed to many blacks. They had watched groups such as the NAACP struggle against these issues with little effect. In the face of the discrimination and joblessness prevalent during the depression, Communist leaders heaped blame for the problems of the times and for inequality itself on such organizations as the NAACP and the National Urban League. As one black Communist leader, Cyril Briggs, proclaimed:

> The Negro bourgeoisie does not put up any real fight against Negro oppression for the reasons that they have a stake in the system that oppresses us. They are lap dogs at the table of the imperialists, demanding simply increased participation ... in the exploitation of the Negro masses.[3]

The ILD and the Communist Party seemed to be *doing* something; they were getting out there in the midst of the melee and actively battling racial prejudice and unjust laws. It was little surprise, therefore, that the ILD should take a keen interest in the group of men and boys that was to become known as the Scottsboro Boys in the spring of 1931. No other case at the time seemed to illustrate so well the injustice of the capitalistic system.

However, the Communist Party was not the only group to become interested in the Scottsboro case.

2
PAINT ROCK, ALABAMA

In 1931, Scottsboro, the county seat of the largely rural county of Jackson, Alabama, was a sleepy town. Once a week the town would rouse to life when the surrounding farmers drove their cars or mule-drawn wagons into town for market day. The Great Depression, however, had laid its heavy fist upon the South and the sharecroppers and farmers of Jackson County felt its weight just as much as those in the teeming cities. Prices for crops and produce were down and the farmers at market grumbled and complained at the few coins their hours of labor brought them.

Twenty miles away, the town of Paint Rock didn't even have the weekly market day to stir it to life. A tiny town, it was only one stop on the route of the Alabama Great Southern Railroad, which slowly wound its way from Chattanooga, Tennessee, down into Alabama and eventually back up into Tennessee to Memphis.

As with other railroads across the country during the 1930s, the Great Southern Railroad's slow-moving freight trains provided free rides to those who moved from place to place seeking jobs. By some estimates, two hundred thousand boys, girls, men, and women made the rails their home. As Haywood Patterson, one of the Scottsboro Boys, later said: "Many freight rides I had by the time I was sixteen. I knew all the nearby states, southeast to Georgia and down to Pensacola, Florida, north to Ohio, west to Arkansas. I knew the train schedules, when the freights left and when they arrived."[1] As a train would slowly start to pull out of a town or city, there would be a rush from bushes, culverts, and behind buildings as the "hoboes" scrambled for a free ride to another town, another chance.

On March 25, 1931, the portrait was the same. Haywood Patterson, Roy and Andy Wright, and Eugene Williams hopped the train in a group; they were all friends, having grown up together on the streets of Chattanooga. Ozie Powell, Clarence Norris, Olen Montgomery, Charlie Weems, and Willie Roberson hailed from different parts of Georgia. Men and boys, they scrambled for the slow-moving freight along with others as it chugged out of the city of Chattanooga.

It was a chilly day, in the upper fifties, but the sun was warm and the sides of the freight cars gave some shelter from the wind. For most of the hitchhikers, it was just going to be another ordinary ride, and they settled themselves as comfortably as they could to wait for it to be over.

Patterson remembers:

The trouble began when three or four white boys crossed over the oil tankers that four of us colored fellows from Chattanooga were in. One of the white boys, he stepped on my hand and liked to have knocked me off the train. I didn't say anything then, but the same guy, he brushed me again and liked to have pushed me off the car.[2]

So Haywood Patterson recalled how the infamous incident started. He complained to the white man who had stepped on his hand and was answered with angry jeers and told to get off the train. Joined by his friends, the white man jumped from the slowly moving train to gather rocks and gravel that they threw at the black men and boys. Shouting names and throwing rocks, the white men ran beside the train. When the black men and boys returned the insults, the white men climbed back onto the train. What had initially been just a shouting match quickly escalated into an all-out brawl on top of the freight cars. As Clarence Norris related:

We fought the white boys and it was a bloody battle. We beat the hell out of them and made 'em get off the train. The ones that didn't want to go we throwed off. We were moving pretty fast, so when they hit the ground they would tumble quite a ways. We let one guy stay because the train started moving too fast for him to make a safe landing.[3]

After all but one of the white men were put off the train, the black men and boys settled down to wait out the ride.

The white men were furious at being thrown from the train. As Haywood Patterson later stated:

> They ran back to Stevenson to complain that they were jumped on and thrown off—and to have us pulled off the train.
> The Stevenson depot man, he called up ahead to Paint Rock and told the folks in that little through-road place to turn out in a posse and snatch us off the train.[4]

Between one and two in the afternoon, Jackson County Deputy Sheriff Charlie Latham received a call in Paint Rock from his superior, Sheriff M. L. Wann. "Capture every negro on the train," Wann told Latham, "and bring them to Scottsboro."[5] Wann also authorized Latham to deputize every white man he could find in Paint Rock.

When the Chattanooga-to-Memphis train slowly pulled into Paint Rock just before two o'clock, the rails were lined with men ominously fingering rifles, shotguns, and axes. Latham ordered them to search the train—all forty-two cars of it. In less than ten minutes, the nine black men and boys, along with the one remaining white man, were rousted out. In addition, the searchers found two white women on the train, both dressed in men's overalls with dresses and other clothes underneath. According to the nine black men and boys who had just been taken from the train, this was their first sight of Victoria Price and Ruby Bates.

Latham questioned the nine blacks, asking what they had been doing on the train. Frightened and surrounded by an increasingly unruly crowd armed to the teeth, the nine mumbled that they had been hitchhiking from Chattanooga in search of work and had not started the trouble. Latham then roped the nine together and loaded them into the back of a truck. He was preparing to have them driven to Scottsboro, the county seat, when the two white women who had been on the train approached him.

In a nervous voice, Ruby Bates told Latham that she and her friend, Victoria Price, had been sexually assaulted by the black men and boys while on the train. To make a charge such as this in the South at that time was akin to lighting a fire in a dry forest. When the surrounding crowd heard the women's charges, there were outcries of rage and yells to "string up" (hang) the nine. The mob surged forward, but Latham prevailed, saying that the nine would go to the jail in Scottsboro, calming the crowd. Deputy Sheriff Latham then took Ruby Bates and Victoria Price with him to Scottsboro. The nine black men and boys were driven off in a truck to the jail there.

In one cell of the Scottsboro jail, the nine men and boys nervously shifted about, getting to know one another, trying to discover what they were being charged with, why they were being held. The four who knew each other were Roy and Andy Wright, thirteen and nineteen years old respectively; twelve-year-old Eugene Williams, and Haywood Patterson, aged nineteen. Charlie Weems, twenty years old, and Clarence Norris, who was in his late teens or early twenties, were both from Georgia, although neither knew the other. All seven had been involved in the fight on the train. Nineteen-year-old Olen Montgomery was completely blind in one eye and nearly so in the other, and Willie Roberson suffered from an untreated venereal disease and could barely walk. Neither Montgomery nor Roberson had taken part in the fight on the train. Nevertheless, all nine would be charged with the same crime. And all nine would be referred to as the Scottsboro Boys. Although some were men, in the South at that time whites called all but elderly black men "boys." They called old black men "uncle."

As the nine huddled in the dirty, ill-lit cage of the Scottsboro jail, they could hear cries from outside: "Bring 'em out!" "Let's string them boys up now!" An angry crowd of white men armed with sticks, pitchforks, and rifles milled around the jail in the twilight. "If you ain't goin' to bring 'em out, we'll come git 'em," cried one man, and the crowd of several hundred surged toward the jail doorway. It was market day in Scottsboro, so the crowd was larger than it ordinarily might have been. When white residents of the town and the visiting farmers and their families heard of the arrest of nine blacks for assaulting two white women, they had all come flocking to the jail with only one thought on their minds: lynching, or mob killing.

"Justice is going to be done," Sheriff Wann called out to the crowd. Hastily deputizing twelve citizens, Wann, with his own nine deputies, barricaded the jailhouse door from the inside. "If you come in here I will blow your brains out. Get away from here," Wann called.[6]

Besieged and realizing that, even with his deputies, he might not be able to hold off the angry mob that was throwing sticks and rocks and bottles, Wann called the Alabama governor, Ben Miller, and asked for help from the Alabama National Guard. Governor Miller wasted no time in sending guardsmen to surround the jailhouse. As Clarence Norris said, "They had to put something on those crackers; they cracked some heads because they wouldn't leave peaceable. After the guard cleared the streets, they stationed themselves outside the jail and all over town. But I didn't get any sleep that night."[7]

The next day, with an uneasy peace lying heavily over the town of Scottsboro, the nine Scottsboro Boys were led from their cell and placed in a lineup. Sheriff Wann then brought in the two women, Victoria Price and Ruby Bates, and asked them to identify all those who had assaulted them. Victoria Price identified six of the Scottsboro Boys and Ruby Bates identified the remaining three. It was at this time that the nine men and boys discovered that they were being accused of sexual assault, and they all began denying the charges loudly and earnestly. "No, sheriff, we didn't do that," Clarence Norris cried out.[8] As he later said, "I knew if a white woman accused a black man of rape, he was as good as dead."[9] And Norris had a firm basis for this belief. In the minds of most southerners at that time, there was no greater crime.

The local newspapers reacted strongly to the identification, reflecting local white sentiment. The "details of the crime coming from the lips of the two girls, Victoria Price and Ruby Bates, are too revolting to be printed and they are being treated by local physicians for injuries sustained when attacked and assaulted by these negroes," stated the *Progressive Age* of March 26, 1931. The *Jackson County Sentinel* of the same date more brazenly blared the headline, "All Negroes Positively Identified by Girls and One White Boy Who Was Held Prisoner with Pistols and Knives While Nine Black Fiends Committed Revolting Crime." According to this article in the *Sentinel*, Victoria Price and Ruby Bates were "found . . . in a terrible condition mentally and physically after their unspeakable experience at the hands of the black brutes." No mention was made of the fact that the women were found in a part of the train quite separate from the section in which the Scottsboro Boys had been riding, nor that Price and Bates had sat under a tree at Paint Rock for some time chatting pleasantly with some of the local women before approaching Deputy Sheriff Latham with their story. Also omitted was the fact that the local physicians who had examined both women could find little evidence of any attack.

As the days passed, the newspapers discovered a gold mine in Victoria Price and in Orville Gilley, the white man who had been on the train and who said he substantiated the two women's story. Victoria Price waxed lyrical over how she had had such a rough life, the only support of a poor, widowed old mother, working in cotton mills to feed the family. She was just on the train, she said, because she and Ruby Bates had gone to Chattanooga to look for honest work and were hitching back to Huntsville, Alabama, their home, to get their belongings. She and Ruby, Victoria said, were brutally held down by the Scottsboro Boys and threatened with knives and guns. Although Ruby Bates was silent during Victoria's many retellings of their lurid tale, only occasionally shooting a stream of tobacco into a nearby spittoon, the Scottsboro citizens were so moved by the plight of these two "flowers of southern womanhood" that they donated new clothing to both.

Orville Gilley had identified all of the Scottsboro Boys as being on the train and, he said, had even seen the actual attack on the two women. He said he himself had been threatened with a pistol by one black man and another had held a knife against his ribs. Gilley was a n'er-do-well transient who rode the rails from town to town, proud of never having worked a day in his life. He earned what little money he had by reciting his own poetry on the streets of the different towns and cities through which he passed.

The nine Scottsboro Boys, meanwhile, were in a frenzy of fear. After being accused, Roy Wright pleaded that he and his brother, Andy, along with Eugene Williams and Haywood Patterson, were blameless and implicated the others. At that point, he would have said anything to free himself and his friends. According to the Scottsboro *Progressive Age* of March 26, 1931, "One of the younger negroes was taken out by himself and he confessed to the whole affair, but said 'the others did it.' "

The other eight Scottsboro Boys merely denied the charges, but Roy Wright's statement was further ammunition for the authorities. Judge Alfred E. Hawkins convened a grand jury the week after the incident. The grand jury swiftly indicted all nine, including Roy Wright, setting the trials to begin on April 6, 1931, only six days after the indictments were handed down. The outcomes of the trials were foregone conclusions, as indicated in an article in the April 2, 1931, *Jackson County Sentinel*: "The evidence against the negroes was so conclusive as to be almost perfect."

Scottsboro and the state of Alabama, however, had been made increasingly aware of the poor public image being presented to the rest of the nation. Newspaper articles appearing in the rest of the country proclaimed the near lynching of the Scottsboro Boys and instantly created sympathy for the nine. Therefore, despite the obvious bias and lynching atmosphere, the Scottsboro Boys were to be given a "fair and lawful trial," as the *Progressive Age* called it, "although the case charged against the negroes appears to be the most revolting in the criminal records of our state, and certainly of our county."

3
"A FAIR
AND LAWFUL
TRIAL"

Judge Alfred E. Hawkins, who would be hearing the
Scottsboro case, looked about for local lawyers who
would be willing to defend the nine Scottsboro Boys.
If the trial was not to be a total sham, the nine must be
defended by counsel. But one by one the local Scottsboro lawyers, when approached, seemed to have pressing reasons why they could not serve as counsel for the
nine. Only one man was willing to handle the case: Milo
C. Moody.

Milo Moody had been admitted to the bar at
Scottsboro in 1889, although he had never completed
college. On April 6, 1931, as the trial commenced, he
was approaching seventy years of age. As one acquaintance noted, Moody was a "doddering, extremely unreliable [and] senile individual who is losing whatever
ability he once had."[1] During his prime, Moody had defended some unpopular causes, but he agreed to defend

the Scottsboro Boys not out of any belief in their innocence, but because the duty earned him a small fee.

Supplementing Moody's dubious abilities were the equally weak skills of Stephen Roddy, a Chattanooga lawyer known for his inability to stay sober. At the pleading of the parents of some of the Scottsboro Boys, a group of black ministers in Chattanooga, the Interdenominational Ministers' Alliance, had hired Roddy to travel to Scottsboro to help the nine. Roddy's legal experience in criminal matters was almost nonexistent, but he agreed to see what he could do for a fee of $120. Although his avowed intent was to see that the nine got a "fair trial," the Scottsboro Boys had little faith in him. "I didn't know what a lawyer was supposed to be," Clarence Norris later wrote, "but I knew this one was no good for us. He had liquor on his breath and he was as scared as we were. When we got into the courtroom and the judge asked him if he was our lawyer, the man said, 'Not exactly.' "[2] Although Roddy participated throughout the first trials of the Scottsboro Boys, he kept reiterating that he was only there to advise. With Moody and Roddy in their corner, the Scottsboro Boys had little hope.

On April 6, 1931, the day the trials of the Scottsboro Boys were to begin, an outsider would have thought the little town was celebrating some great festival. Bands played, people flocked to the town from the surrounding hills and countryside, neighboring counties, and even neighboring states. All wanted to watch the famous trial, and by early morning several thousand people were trying to get to the courthouse through the National Guard picket lines.

In the courtroom itself, the seats reserved for onlookers were packed with a crowd eager to see the show. After determining that Roddy and Moody were defending the Scottsboro Boys, Judge Hawkins ruled on a motion by Roddy for a change of venue, a change of the location of the trials. The inflammatory nature of the newspaper stories, Roddy argued, had biased opinion against the nine. While Roddy's contention was a very sound one, he had not adequately prepared it, having arranged for no witnesses to appear to support it. The prosecutor called Sheriff Wann, who the week before had found it necessary to call in the National Guard because of unruly public "sentiment." The sheriff now testified that he felt nothing would stand in the way of the nine getting a fair trial. He was supported in this claim by Major Joseph Starnes of the National Guard, who claimed that the enormous crowd even then surrounding the courthouse was there because of "curiosity" rather than to threaten the defendants.

Judge Hawkins quickly denied Roddy's motion to change the trial's location. From this point on, any attempt to defend the Scottsboro Boys by Roddy or Moody was mere formality. In fact, Moody had publicly stated to the press that the assignment to defend them was "distasteful" to him. There was, in essence, to be no defense.

The prosecution was handled by Circuit Solicitor H. G. Bailey, who expected Roddy and Moody to ask for separate trials for the nine men and boys. Surprisingly, Roddy said he had no objection to all nine being tried together. Bailey, however, suggested that there be four trials: Clarence Norris and Charlie Weems would be tried together; then Haywood Patterson alone; then Olen Montgomery, Ozie Powell, Willie Roberson, Andy Wright, and Eugene Williams; lastly, Roy Wright. Bailey did not explain his reasons for separating the trials in this manner. Judge Hawkins agreed to this motion, and by 2:30 in the afternoon of the same day, a jury had been chosen, and the first trial, of Norris and Weems, was under way.

Bailey first called Victoria Price to the stand. Dressed in a new dress and without her usual chaw of tobacco, Victoria Price bluntly told of boarding the train, watching the fight between the white men and the black men and boys, and then being overpowered by the nine Scottsboro Boys and assaulted. Clarence Norris wrote: "They [Price and Bates] said we used knives and hit them up the side of the head with guns. . . . But the law never found no knives or guns on us because we didn't have any."[3]

Roddy tried to discredit Price's account by claiming that she was hardly the creature of high morals she claimed to be. He had learned from Dr. R. R. Bridges of Jackson County, one of the two doctors who had examined Price and Bates after the alleged attack, that although there was evidence that the two women had had sexual relations prior to the supposed attack, there were few of the bruises and lacerations that were the usual indications of rape. (A later investigation of Price's character and background, conducted by a freelance writer hired by the American Civil Liberties Union [ACLU], served to bear out Roddy's claim: a deputy sheriff in Huntsville, Alabama, confided that Price was a "quiet prostitute" who "just took men quiet-like.")

In answer to Roddy's questions, Price admitted that she had been married twice, was separated from her second husband, and had always used her maiden name, even when she was married. But when Roddy attempted to probe more deeply into her past, Prosecutor Bailey objected, and Judge Hawkins ruled that the defense could not use that line of attack. The characters of Victoria Price and Ruby Bates were not to be questioned.

Bailey then called Dr. Bridges to the stand. The doctor testified that there was no evidence of the bruising, hitting, and manhandling that Price and Bates claimed to have experienced. He said that "Victoria Price was not hysterical at all at that time."[4] He added, however, that his examination of the woman showed evidence of recent sexual relations and that they *could* have been attacked. That was enough for the jury and Judge Hawkins. Dr. Bridges's testimony was supported by that of a second physician, Dr. Marvin Lynch, who had also examined the girls. After this testimony, Judge Hawkins adjourned the court for the day.

The next day, April 7, was marked by the testimony of Ruby Bates. Unlike Victoria Price, who had matter-of-factly told her story, dramatically embellishing it with accounts of cocked guns and threatening knives, Ruby

Bates seemed unsure of herself. Pausing frequently, she hesitantly confirmed Price's account of the events. Roddy did not question Ruby Bates about the inconsistencies between her story and Price's, but only brought out the fact that neither she nor Price had mentioned the assault to the posse when the train had first pulled into Paint Rock and had been searched.

Other witnesses for the state consisted of farmers and Paint Rock citizens. They said that they had seen the fight on the train as it had passed their lands. One, Luther Morris, stated that he was standing in the loft of his barn as the train passed and saw some black men "put off five white men and take charge of two girls."[5] The Chattanooga *Daily Times* declared Morris's testimony to be "the most damaging evidence against the Negroes." With this damning testimony, the prosecutor rested his case.

Roddy and Moody had no witnesses to present except the Scottsboro Boys themselves, most of whom denied attacking or even seeing the two women on the train. "I don't know where the girls were," Charlie Weems asserted in his testimony. "There wasn't a soul in that car with me and Patterson except those Negroes and one white boy. . . . I never saw no girls in this gondola which we were in at all. . . . I never saw anything done to the girls."[6]

When Norris took the stand, however, he tried to save himself. He said that all the other Scottsboro Boys had attacked the girls; he alone had not participated; he alone was innocent. With one blow, Norris shattered

Roddy's already feeble defense of the Scottsboro Boys. During a courtroom break, Roddy tried to salvage what little he could. He tried to get Bailey to accept a guilty plea from his clients in exchange for a sentence of life in prison, rather than the death penalty. Confident in the strength of his case, Bailey refused to bargain. When the court reconvened, Roddy, unable to get Norris to change his testimony, rested his case. Although Roddy and Moody declined to present any closing arguments to the jury, Bailey did, calling for the death penalty for Weems and Norris.

Approximately twenty-four hours after the first trial of Clarence Norris and Charlie Weems had begun, it was sent to the jury for deliberation. Within two hours, while the trial of Haywood Patterson was under way, the jury notified the court that they had reached a decision. A halt was called in Patterson's trial, the jurors for Weems and Norris replaced those for Patterson in the jury box, and the foreman announced, "We find the defendants guilty of rape and fix their sentence at death in—" But before the foreman could finish, roars, cheers, and whistles from the courtroom crowd drowned him out. The cheers were taken up by those waiting outside the courthouse as the news reached them, rocking the courthouse with shouts, hurrahs, and whistles. Judge Hawkins pounded his gavel for quiet with no result. Finally the judge ordered the National Guard to quiet those in the courtroom and a sort of jubilant order was restored.

Roddy, scrambling after the slightest thread to bolster

his defense of Haywood Patterson, whose trial was then under way, claimed that the crowd noises had biased Patterson's jury, which had been in another room yet could hear the commotion. Roddy called for a mistrial, citing a 1919 Supreme Court decision ruling in favor of two black defendants because the jury had been influenced "by an irresistible wave of public passion."[7] Judge Hawkins, however, denied Roddy's motion after questioning the jury members, who said that, although they had heard the noise, it had not influenced them. The trial of Haywood Patterson proceeded.

In most respects, Haywood Patterson's trial echoed that of Norris and Weems. Patterson, however, had a disadvantage they'd not had. As a boy, he had gotten into trouble with the Chattanooga police. His prior record, as well as his insolent attitude, turned the jury against him. Although Roddy called Patterson's four friends, who had been traveling with him, to testify in support of his story of innocence, he, too, was quickly found guilty and sentenced to death. "I went on trial about nine o'clock in the morning," Patterson later wrote in his account, *Scottsboro Boy*. "Within two hours the jury had come back with a conviction. I was convicted in their minds before I went on trial. . . . All that spoke for me on that witness stand was my black skin—which didn't do so good."[8]

The trials of the remaining men and boys followed similar patterns, with the exception of Roy Wright's. Roy Wright was just thirteen years old and under Alabama law could only be tried in a juvenile court unless the state moved to waive this requirement. Bailey tried to get Roddy to agree to a waiver in exchange for a sentence of life imprisonment but Roddy refused. So Roy Wright was tried as a juvenile. Oddly enough, Eugene Williams also claimed to be twelve years old, but he was not believed. By April 9, all the defendants had been found guilty except Roy Wright. His jury was hopelessly tied up over whether he should be given life imprisonment or the death penalty and, reluctantly, Judge Hawkins declared a mistrial in his case. This did not mean, however, that Roy Wright was freed; he was sent back to jail to await a new trial.

Late in the afternoon of the same day, April 9, Judge Hawkins called all the defendants except Roy Wright before him. "It is the judgment of the court," Hawkins intoned, "and the sentence of the law that the defendants be sentenced to death by electrocution at Kilby Prison in the City of Montgomery, Montgomery County, Alabama, on Friday the 10th day of July, 1931."[9]

For the eight standing before Judge Hawkins the future appeared short and bleak. Yet even as Hawkins pronounced sentence, efforts on behalf of the Scottsboro Boys were under way throughout the country. A few hours after sentencing, Judge Hawkins and Governor Ben Miller of Alabama each received an identical telegram from the International Labor Defense of the American Communist Party. The telegrams read:

WE DEMAND STAY OF EXECUTION AND OPPORTUNITY TO INVESTIGATE AND PREPARE FOR NEW TRIAL OR APPEAL. WE DEMAND RIGHT FOR OUR ATTORNEY TO INTERVIEW DEFENDANTS AND TO OBTAIN FORMAL APPROVAL OF DEFENSE COUNSEL. AND, ABOVE ALL, WE DEMAND ABSOLUTE SAFETY FOR THE DEFENDANTS AGAINST LYNCHING.[10]

4
"LET THOSE PORE BOYS GET FREE"

Black and white men and women across the country had closely followed the trials of the Scottsboro Boys. Letters supporting the nine men and boys from every region and from every social level of the United States flooded into Alabama. A black woman who lived in New York wrote to Governor Miller pleading with him to "let those pore boys get free." A lawyer from Atlanta, Georgia, wrote, "I can understand how such savagery can exist in a state like Mississippi . . . but I refuse to believe that a civilized community like that of your state will be guilty of such an atrocity."[1] The nation was stunned by the blatant injustice of the trials and the sentencing to death of the Scottsboro Boys.

Because of the American Communist Party's avowed interest in recruiting black members and in promoting racial equality, the Scottsboro case was of great importance to it from the start, and the party moved to make it a focus of its anti-lynching crusade. It immediately organized protests and letter-writing campaigns, publicized the case in its newspaper, the *Daily Worker*, and arranged for the parents of the Scottsboro Boys to travel nationally and internationally on speaking tours. The party also sent International Labor Defense lawyers to help the Scottsboro Boys.

Founded in 1925 by the Communist Party to counteract the activities of such organizations as the Ku Klux Klan, the International Labor Defense was a group of attorneys that claimed independence from the Communist Party. But this claim was merely a way to attract prominent liberal attorneys to its cause. No noncommunist was ever a major leader in the organization.

But with the entrance into the case of the ILD, there arose a controversy between the ILD and the NAACP.

Always cautious and protective of its public image, the NAACP had hesitated to step forward to defend the Scottsboro Boys. As historian Dan Carter has pointed out, "The last thing they [the NAACP] wanted was to identify the Association with a gang of mass rapists unless they were reasonably certain the boys were innocent or their constitutional rights were abridged."[2] Pushed by public pressure after the sentencings of the Scottsboro Boys, the NAACP's executive secretary, Walter White, moved to obtain copies of the trial transcripts for study, relying on the Chattanooga Ministers' Alliance—and through them, Stephen Roddy—to obtain them for him. On April 22, thirteen days after the trials, White was still awaiting the transcripts. It was then he discovered in a telephone call to Alabama that Stephen Roddy had not gotten them because he refused to pay the transcription costs. Only after the NAACP sent a check to Scottsboro did the organization receive the transcripts. The delay had been costly.

While the NAACP was dragging its heels, the ILD had been on the move, sending two of its lawyers, Allan Traub and Joseph R. Brodsky, to Scottsboro to visit the Scottsboro Boys, who were then being held in the Jefferson County Jail awaiting transfer to Kilby Prison and death row. In order not to arouse the citizens of Scottsboro, "they told the guards they had come from Tuscaloosa, Alabama," according to Clarence Norris, "to see those 'Scottsboro niggers.' They looked like farmers and talked like rednecks."[3] Once alone with the Scottsboro Boys, however, Traub and Brodsky assured them that they were there to help and that appeals would be requested on all their sentences.

But promising something and doing it are often two very different things. While the ILD pursued the defense of the Scottsboro Boys, they were also clashing with the NAACP, which, likewise, wished to control the Scottsboro cases. On April 18, representatives of the ILD spoke before the Chattanooga Ministers' Alliance, assuring them of their good intentions and of the fact that the ILD would assume all costs of the Scottsboro appeals by holding fund-raisers. The ILD had previously approached Stephen Roddy about continuing on the case, but he was reluctant to do so (he later changed his mind). Therefore the ILD hired George W. Chamlee, Sr., as their local attorney and liaison because of his known willingness to defend Communists in the South. Chamlee met with the Scottsboro Boys, who agreed to sign an affidavit turning the case over to the ILD.

When Walter White heard of the ILD's actions, he urged his local representative in Alabama, Dr. P. A. Stephens, a member of the Chattanooga Ministers' Alliance, to meet with the Scottsboro Boys and urge them to repudiate their affidavit. Stephens convinced Roddy to talk with the nine and get them to sign a statement telling the ILD to "lay off."

From this point on, it was tug and pull between the NAACP and the ILD as to who would defend the Scottsboro Boys and control the appeals process. While the nine men and boys waited anxiously in prison, they were urged by lawyers, parents, and relatives to go first one way, then another. The NAACP, spearheaded by Walter White, argued that their aim was to guarantee the Boys a fair trial in the Alabama courts, which could only be assured if the defense hired local attorneys and avoided actions that antagonized Alabama public opinion. "Communist involvement in the case," Walter White declared, would only "hamper the proper conduct of the defense."[4]

The ILD, for its part, countered by, first, attempting to get the defendants' approval of their handling of the case and, second, trying to publicly discredit the NAACP and its efforts. The ILD enlisted the support of the Boys' parents by having the parents write to the nine and by driving a number of them to the prison so they could convince their sons to let the ILD represent them. In addition, to ease the onus of prison, the ILD arranged for the Scottsboro Boys to receive a small amount of money: "Each of us got a check from the Communists for eight dollars a month," wrote Clarence Norris, "and three dollars from the NAACP."[5]

In their campaign on behalf of the Scottsboro Boys, the ILD organized rallies and marches around the country. They brought Haywood Patterson's mother, Janie Patterson, to New York City to give speeches against the "Alabama boss-lynchers." Her appearance was followed by that of ILD supporter Frank Alexander, who inflamed the crowds with his rhetoric. The April 26 headline in the *New York Times* blared, "Police Clubs Rout 200 Defiant Reds Who Attacked 'Lynch Law' in Alabama." Because this and other meetings got so much attention from the press, people came to associate the ILD with the Scottsboro Boys' defense.

The legitimacy of ILD participation was accidentally strengthened by the NAACP itself. On April 24, 1931, the *Daily Worker* printed a letter from William Pickens, the field secretary for the NAACP in Kansas City. Unaware of the struggle going on between the NAACP and the ILD, Pickens wrote in support of the ILD's efforts, urging people to send money to support those efforts and the ILD. The NAACP was stunned by the publication of Pickens's letter and could only answer with half-hearted attacks on the ILD.

Meanwhile, Judge Hawkins announced that on May 7,

1931, he would hear arguments on the motions for new trials for the Scottsboro Boys. Walter White and the NAACP quickly retained the services of a Birmingham firm of lawyers, Fort, Beddow and Ray, of which Roderick Beddow, a junior member, would handle the case. Despite his agreement to handle the case for the NAACP, Beddow preferred to remain in the background, once again leaving the arguments to the inadequate Moody and Roddy.

On June 5, 1931, after two postponements, Judge Hawkins was ready to hear requests for new trials. Before the motions could be presented, he was asked to rule as to which group—the NAACP lawyers or the ILD lawyers, all of whom were present—should be the primary defense team. Roddy said he would work with any lawyer but didn't need "assistance from New York."[6] Judge Hawkins, not wanting to entangle himself in the controversy, ruled that this was a matter for the defendants to decide. As a result, all the lawyers present were permitted to participate in the hearing.

According to the *Jackson County Sentinel*, both the ILD and NAACP attorneys "contended that the trial, conducted with a mob outside, deprived the defendants of their rights under the due process clause of the Fourteenth Amendment to the Constitution." The juries had been influenced both by the presence of the crowds and by the crowds' response to the various verdicts, which could be heard even though the juries had been sent away so as not to hear them. Chamlee and Brodsky of the ILD also submitted a number of signed statements attesting to the bad reputations of both Victoria Price and Ruby Bates.

Those statements were hotly attacked by both the state's assistant attorney and the press. The *Jackson County Sentinel* called them a "filthy attack upon two white girls and supplied by negroes of the lowest class." The paper announced that it was astounded that the statements "would be given credency by anyone." The state's attorney portrayed Price and Bates as two innocent young girls. To claim that the two girls and the lives they had led had been less than perfect was offensive.

Between the attacks of the press and the claims of the state attorneys, public sentiment in Fort Payne, where the hearing was held, was strongly against both the Scottsboro Boys and their lawyers, particularly the ILD lawyers. As Brodsky and Chamlee left the courthouse the night of June 4, they were met by a group of men who quietly but firmly escorted them out of town and told them to stay out.

Despite the fact that the ILD attorneys were thrown out of town for their attack on southern femininity, the crowds had little factual evidence to support their actions. The American Civil Liberties Union had, earlier, released its own investigation of Price and Bates, revealing the tawdry backgrounds of both. A similar investigation by the Commission on Interracial Cooperation, a southern-based organization, substantiated the ACLU's findings. Both, however, tended to be ignored by the locals and the press.

Emotions on all sides were running high. There was a fresh attack on the ILD by the NAACP, which claimed the ILD was using the defense of the Scottsboro Boys as a way of spreading communism throughout the South. The defendants could not receive a fair trial because of this, the NAACP stated. Although the ILD answered in kind, the attack was generally ignored by the papers, which chose instead to express anger at the claim that the Scottsboro Boys would not receive a fair trial. By May 21, 1931, the Scottsboro Boys were roughly split into two camps. Andy and Roy Wright, Haywood Patterson, Eugene Williams, and Olen Montgomery chose to be defended by the ILD. Ozie Powell, Charlie Weems, and Clarence Norris went with the NAACP. Willie Roberson couldn't make up his mind, choosing first one group of lawyers, then the other. Meanwhile, pending appeals of the convictions, on June 22, 1931, Judge Hawkins set aside the execution date that had been hanging over the heads of eight of the nine Scottsboro Boys.

In August, the NAACP's lawyer, Roderick Beddow, attempted once more to convince the nine men and boys that they should all be represented by his firm. Facing division yet again, Walter White urged the famous lawyer Clarence Darrow to accept the case, hoping this would sway those of the Scottsboro Boys who were still united with the ILD.

One of the best known attorneys in the nation, Darrow was in his seventies and had a long and distinguished career defending "the underdog." His most famous trial appearance had been in the Scopes evolution case in 1925. In that case, he had defended a Tennessee schoolteacher charged with violating a state law that prohibited teaching evolution. William Jennings Bryan, an equally famous attorney, had prosecuted the case against Darrow's client. While Darrow had lost the case, his tactic of putting Bryan on the witness stand and his skillful questioning of Bryan did much to challenge literal interpretation of the Bible.

A strong opponent of the death penalty, Darrow had defended more than one hundred persons accused of murder, and none of his clients was ever sentenced to death. Walter White believed that Darrow's fame and his reputation for success in defending people accused of capital offenses would attract the Scottsboro Boys away from the ILD.

In response, the ILD moved to strengthen its hold on the nine defendants by persuading their parents that the ILD offered the Boys the best representation. As a result of these efforts on the part of the ILD, Clarence Norris, Ozie Powell, and Charlie Weems dismissed their NAACP attorneys and put their fates in the hands of the ILD's lawyers.

A meeting of all the lawyers, including Clarence Darrow, resulted in a stalemate. The ILD would accept Darrow and Arthur Hays, another NAACP lawyer, but only if they withdrew as NAACP attorneys and issued a "public statement [to] that effect." Faced by this ultimatum, Darrow and Hays chose to withdraw from the case and, on January 4, 1932, the NAACP announced its own decision to withdraw from the case completely. Regardless of what the Scottsboro Boys might or might not have wished, they were left with the lawyers of the ILD after being innocently caught between clashing forces and ideologies for nearly a year. Ignorant as the nine were of these forces and of the law, they were held to blame. In January, Walter White wrote to Charlie Weems: "You and the other boys have vacillated, changing your minds so frequently that it is impossible for any organization or individual to know just what you do want."[7]

5

POWELL V. ALABAMA

With the NAACP out of the Scottsboro case, the ILD proceeded quickly with the appeals process, despite having to face local distaste toward its involvement. The Birmingham *News* declared that the ILD's defense of the Scottsboro Boys was disruptive to race relations, adding, "In these troubled times, some blacks may be tempted to follow after false prophets." In spite of its lack of public approval and the mire of its own ideology, the ILD began to prepare its appeal of the cases to the Alabama Supreme Court.

The ILD lawyers, with local lawyer George Chamlee, Sr., advising, had no great hope of success with the Alabama Supreme Court. As Chamlee admitted in a letter to a colleague on December 8, 1931, "Officers at Scottsboro and court officials there think we have not got a ghost of a chance and that our case is just hopeless and impossible."[1] The ILD did not despair, however; they viewed this appeal as only one step in a legal process that would lead eventually to the United States Supreme Court.

The hearing began on January 21, 1932, with ILD lawyer Joseph Brodsky presenting most of the arguments for the Scottsboro Boys. Brodsky's defense focused on a number of issues. First, since Alabama juries did not include blacks, Brodsky argued that they were not juries of the defendants' peers nor representative of the population as a whole. A second argument focused on Roy Wright's trial and Judge Hawkins's decision to try him despite the fact that Wright should have been tried in a juvenile court. (Although Wright had been tried as a juvenile, Hawkins's court was not a juvenile court.) As Brodsky stated in the *New York Times*, January 23, 1932, this "illustrated the speed and pressure of these trials and that the minds of the men [in charge] were not normal." Brodsky's main argument, however, focused on the issue of a fair trial. He argued that the jury had been biased both by newspaper accounts and by the crowds at the trial and that the nine men and boys had a right to be heard by a jury "entirely free from bias or prejudice, and free from outside or extralegal influences which might distract their minds from a dispassionate consideration of the merits of the case."

George Chamlee spoke on one issue: the inadequacy of the Boys' defense counsel. At no time before the trials had commenced in Scottsboro had the nine men and boys been permitted to consult with an attorney. At the trial itself, Chamlee pointed out, Stephen Roddy had repeatedly said he was not hired to represent the nine and

Judge Hawkins had treated the entire matter of adequate counsel in a most offhand manner.

The next day, January 22, the state presented its arguments. As Clarence Norris later noted: "The attorney general of Alabama, Thomas G. Knight, Jr., appeared for the state. His daddy, Thomas G. Knight, Sr., was one of the judges on the court."[2] Paying little attention to the charges of inadequate counsel or the jury issue, Knight focused on the idea that the juries had been unduly influenced. But, "Why should we assume," he asked, "that the gathering of a curious mob would have influenced the jurors and judge of the trial court?"[3]

Although the ILD lawyers had argued eloquently, the result was predictable. On March 24, 1932, the Alabama Supreme Court upheld the decisions of the lower court, with the exception of the conviction of Eugene Williams. Williams was granted a new trial because he was only twelve years old at the time of his trial and should have been tried as a juvenile. The court decision even questioned his true age, saying that the claims that he was now thirteen years old "may be false."

The issue of whether there should have been blacks on the jury was brushed off. "The State of Alabama," Justice Thomas Knight, Sr., wrote in the court's decision, "has the right, within constitutional limitations, to fix the qualifications for jurors." A new date was also set for the execution of seven of the Scottsboro Boys: Haywood Patterson, Andy Wright, Olen Montgomery, Clarence Norris, Willie Roberson, Charlie Weems, and Ozie Powell. As previously noted, Roy Wright was being held for trial as a minor. This date was later set aside pending appeal to the United States Supreme Court.

Local citizens greeted the Alabama Supreme Court's decision with jubilation. The trials *were* fair, they pointed out, the court said so. The court's decision salved any doubts Alabamians might have secretly harbored about the Scottsboro trials. But the rest of the country did not view the decision in this light. To them, the decision merely heaped injustice upon injustice, and letters in support of the Scottsboro Boys again poured forth.

Confronted with one of the greatest legal challenges a lawyer can face—arguing before the United States Supreme Court—the ILD hired Walter Pollak, a constitutional attorney of great renown, to prepare and argue further appeals for the cases. On May 27, 1932, Pollak presented the initial arguments and the Supreme Court ruled that it would review the case.

Presenting a case to the United States Supreme Court first requires attorneys to convince the Court that the case should be reviewed at all. To do this, attorneys must demonstrate that an issue concerning the Constitution is involved in the case. Merely getting the Court to review the Scottsboro case was a triumph for the ILD. Next, attorneys for the Scottsboro Boys and for the state of Alabama went over the case before the Court, pointing out what constitutional issues were involved and why the decision of the lower court should or should not be overturned. In the fall of 1932, Pollak succinctly argued the Scottsboro cases before the Supreme Court.

In essence, he presented the same arguments that Brodsky and Chamlee had placed before the Alabama Supreme Court. Again he brought up the jury question and the fact that the Scottsboro Boys were "young, ignorant, illiterate blacks who were convicted and sentenced to death without effective appointment of counsel to aid them."[4] Finally, Pollak argued, the trials were not fair, impartial or deliberate; the jury had been influenced by the mobs and the newspaper coverage. Thomas G. Knight, Jr.'s, arguments against these charges were weak and defensive. He must have realized how poorly the facts of the Scottsboro cases stood up to scrutiny outside his home state of Alabama.

On Monday, November 7, 1932, rumor circulated around Washington, D.C., that the Supreme Court was ready to issue its decision. A crowd gathered before the Supreme Court building carrying placards in support of the Scottsboro Boys. After repeated requests by the police to disperse, they rioted.

Despite the melee outside the Court, inside the atmosphere was calm. Justice George Sutherland read the decision: the Scottsboro judgments were annulled. New trials were to be ordered for the Scottsboro Boys. The ILD had triumphed.

The Court had discounted the jury question and focused upon whether the defendants had been properly defended. In the decision, Sutherland wrote:

> It is hardly necessary to say that the right to counsel being conceded, a defendant should be

afforded a fair opportunity to secure counsel of his own choice. Not only was that not done here, but such designation of counsel as was attempted was either so indefinite or so close upon the trial as to amount to a denial of effective and substantial aid in that regard. . . . Under the circumstances disclosed we hold that defendants were not accorded the right of counsel in any substantial sense. To decide otherwise would simply be to ignore actualities.[5]

The Court ruled under the "due process" clause of the Fourteenth Amendment to the Constitution, rather than under the Sixth Amendment's "right to counsel" clause, because the Sixth Amendment refers to federal courts, not state courts. According to the decision, the Court, because of the Constitution, had a duty to "regulate the administration of criminal justice by the states" and to see that a fair trial was held. In the Scottsboro cases, because the lawyers came into the case late, and one (Roddy) was unfamiliar with Alabama law, there was a failure of due process.

The *New York Times* celebrated the landmark nature of the *Powell v. Alabama* decision and remarked that it reaffirmed the soundness of the Constitution. In Kilby Prison in Alabama, the Scottsboro Boys celebrated, too. "On November 8, 1932," Haywood Patterson wrote, "the boys shouted, they were so glad. Andy Wright, from his cell, read out loud that we fellows won a new trial."[6]

There was hope for the Scottsboro Boys after all!

Olen Montgomery wrote on behalf of all the Scottsboro Boys to thank the ILD: "Since the Supreme Court have granted we boys a new trial I thank it is my rite to express thanks and appreciation to the whole party for their care. . . . I myself feels like I have been born again from the worrying . . . I have had."[7]

Being on death row and in Kilby Prison had had a depressing effect upon the Scottsboro Boys. Although they received small amounts of money to buy cigarettes and candy, they were not permitted to exercise, there being no exercise yard for the death row inmates, and the medical facilities were nearly nonexistent. "The guards hated us," Clarence Norris wrote, "because of all the attention we got from the outside world. They came into our cells and abused us at will. . . . They made us parade buck naked from our cells to the bath twice a week. . . . This was special treatment just for us."[8] Other of the Scottsboro Boys reported being harassed and beaten by the guards for infractions that were overlooked when other prisoners committed them. To many Alabamians, including the guards at Kilby Prison, black men had no rights, and the Supreme Court had no right telling white people how they should run their affairs in their state.

With the Supreme Court decision and the scheduling of new trials for March 1933, the outlook for the Scottsboro Boys seemed greatly improved, although their treatment in prison worsened. Their future was temporarily brightened, too, by two additional events. In early 1933, Judge Hawkins at last granted the ILD's

request for a change of venue, and in January 1933 a
letter surfaced in which Ruby Bates purportedly told her
boyfriend that the attack by the Scottsboro Boys never
happened:

> Dearest Earl:
>   I want to make a statement too you. Mary San-
> ders is a goddam lie about those Negroes jazzing
> me those policemen made me tell a lie that is my
> statement because I want to clear myself that is
> all too if you want to believe me OK. If not that
> is okay. You will be sorry some day if you had
> too stay in jail with eight Negroes you would tell
> a lie two those Negroes did not touch me or those
> white boys I hope you will believe me the law
> don't, i love you better than Mary does or any-
> body else in the world that is why I am telling
> you of this thing i was drunk at the time and did
> not know what i was doing i know it was wrong
> too let those Negroes die on account of me i hope
> you will believe my statement because it is the
> gods truth i hope you will believe me i was jazzed
> but those white boys jazzed me i wish those Ne-
> groes are not Burnt on account of me it is those
> white boys fault that is my statement, and that is
> all I know i hope you tell the law hope you will
> answer.
>
> Ruby Bates[9]

Ruby Bates, after writing this letter in Huntsville, Alabama, gave it to a friend, Miron Pearlman, to deliver to
"Earl." Along the way, however, Pearlman got into a

fight. He was arrested and the letter was found in his possession.

When the ILD attorneys discovered the existence of the letter, they immediately demanded a copy. However, by that time Ruby Bates was denying its truth. Pearlman told the Huntsville police that George Chamlee had paid him to "get her drunk and have her write a letter to one of her fellows stating that the negroes did not attack her or assault her." Ruby Bates then substantiated Pearlman's account: "I was so drunk that I did not know what I was doing."[10] The letter was never authenticated.

Chamlee denied any role in the affair, although he did know Pearlman. Stephen Roddy, still smarting over being pushed out of the Scottsboro cases and being labeled "inadequate," filed charges with the Chattanooga Bar Association calling for Chamlee's disbarment. Chamlee was found innocent, however, and the charges were dropped by the bar association, but the doubt it left in the public's mind shadowed the upcoming trials and called into question Bates's letter, which could have proven the innocence of the Scottsboro Boys.

Under these circumstances, the Scottsboro Boys were transferred to the Birmingham jail. There they would await their second "fair trial."

6
ANOTHER
"FAIR TRIAL"

William L. Patterson, executive secretary of the ILD, knew that if the second trials of the Scottsboro Boys were to be won, the young defendants would need the best legal counsel available. After the Supreme Court decision was handed down, Patterson approached a New York attorney, Samuel Leibowitz, to take on the cases. However, Patterson told him that the ILD could not pay him anything more than expenses, there being no funds available.

Leibowitz, who upon the retirement of Clarence Darrow had taken up the mantle of being the most effective criminal lawyer in the United States, was willing to take the case. The Scottsboro case, he wrote to Patterson, "touches no controversial theory of economy or government, but the basic rights of man." Wanting to distance himself a bit from the ILD and the Communist Party, however, he added that he was convinced that the people of Alabama would live up to their "great heritage of honor, and to those brave and chivalrous generations of the past, in whose blood the history of the State is written."[1] Leibowitz knew that the people of Alabama bitterly resented the ILD's intervention in the Scottsboro cases and wished to disassociate himself from the ILD in order to be more effective. Although Patterson was not happy with this position, he was willing to tolerate it because of Leibowitz's proven skill.

One ploy Leibowitz decided to use in the trials was to discredit the testimony of Victoria Price and Ruby Bates by investigating their backgrounds, something that earlier lawyers had attempted but had not been permitted to do by Judge Hawkins. "They got depositions and affidavits," wrote Clarence Norris, "from people who swore the women were prostitutes."[2] Leibowitz's investigations revealed the same thing that others had found earlier: the two girls were unreliable witnesses and of questionable moral character. Although technically this information was inadmissible as evidence, it could be used to manipulate the jury and cast doubt on the girls' story.

With the change of venue, the trials would now be held in Decatur, Alabama, a small town of around fifteen thousand people fifty miles west of Scottsboro. Having sought to have the trial shifted to Birmingham, the defense lawyers were upset over the choice of Decatur. One ILD attorney, Irving Schwab, noted, "They are the same class of people there [as in Scottsboro]."[3] Attorney General Thomas Knight, representing the prosecution, disagreed, reiterating the now tired theme that the change of venue would assure that the Scottsboro Boys got a "fair trial." The trials would begin March 27, 1933, with Judge James Edwin Horton, Jr., presiding.

In early March, the Scottsboro Boys were transferred from the Birmingham jail to the Decatur jail. "The Decatur jail was a hellhole," according to Clarence Norris. "It was declared unfit for white prisoners over a year before we got there. But the state thought it was all right for 'niggers.' It was filthy, dust everywhere, big holes were in the floors and walls, plaster fell down around our heads, the stink was sickening and rats the size of rabbits had the run of the place. But the bedbugs! There were millions of them."[4]

Haywood Patterson was the first to be tried. Leibowitz, aided by Chamlee and Brodsky, began with a motion to Judge Horton that the 1931 convictions be overturned as there were no blacks on the jury rolls in Jackson County, where Scottsboro was located. Citing the Supreme Court decision in *Strauder v. West Virginia* (1880) that ruled that "deliberate exclusion of Negroes from the jury lists was a violation of the equal protection clause of the Fourteenth Amendment," Leibowitz argued that the Scottsboro Boys had been denied fair trials. Although Leibowitz, in examining witnesses, showed that no blacks were on the jury rolls in either Scottsboro or Decatur and that many blacks lived in the area who would be qualified to sit on a jury, Judge Horton overruled the motion. Leibowitz had expected this, having posed the motion for the purpose of aiding further appeals should they prove necessary.

The motion and the questioning of witnesses had the effect of antagonizing the white spectators in the courtroom and in Decatur itself. Who was this Leibowitz, they asked, to come down here from New York City and criticize them? Threats to run Leibowitz out of town were so prevalent that Judge Horton took it upon himself to issue a warning against any action: "It is our duty to mete out even handed justice. . . . No other course is open to you . . . and let no one think they can act otherwise than in this manner."[5] As an added precaution, National Guard troops were stationed in the town to assure that no illegal action was taken against the defense lawyers or the Scottsboro Boys.

When the trial began in Decatur that Monday, March 27, the spectator sections of the courtroom were jammed with eager onlookers, and more crowds milled outside the courthouse. The first witness to take the stand against Haywood Patterson was Victoria Price. Once again she smoothly told her story. The surprise came when Attorney General Knight suddenly pulled a torn pair of women's underwear from his briefcase and asked Price if they were hers. Leibowitz was on his feet in a second, loudly objecting: "This is the first time in two years any such step-ins have ever been shown in any court of justice."[6] Then, according to Haywood Patterson, "the attorney general picked them up and said, 'Well, they're here now,' and he tossed them plonk into the face of one of the jurors."[7] This created a furor in the courtroom, but over Leibowitz's objections—and the laughter of the spectators—Judge Horton ruled the "step-ins" to be acceptable evidence.

When Leibowitz attempted to cross-examine Price, she proved surly and unresponsive, saying only things such as, "I ain't sure" and "I would say—I ain't positive," and only reiterating the charge of assault against Patterson and the others. Leibowitz had had an exact replica of the train, the scene of the alleged crime, constructed by the Lionel Corporation, makers of toy trains. But when questioned regarding where on the train she and Ruby Bates had been, and asked to point it out on the model, Price refused to cooperate, saying only: "That is not the train I was on. It was bigger, lots bigger, that is a toy."[8]

Leibowitz then brought up Price's past, but when questioned, Price merely repeating her earlier statements with an "appalling hardness," according to one onlooker. Rather than discredit the witness in the eyes of the jury, Leibowitz's tough cross-examination of Price only seemed to gain her sympathy. "Too late the chief defense attorney realized that Mrs. Price had become the symbol of white Southern womanhood," as Dan T. Carter notes in *Scottsboro: A Tragedy of the American South*.[9]

The last witness for the state on the first day of the trial was Dr. R. R. Bridges, who had examined both Price and Bates not more than two hours after the supposed assault had occurred. As at the earlier trials, the doctor admitted that neither supposed victim had shown any signs of hysteria or upset and that the physical evidence was not there to support their claims. But, he contended, still, he believed the assaults had taken place.

The next day, Dr. Marvin Lynch, the second doctor to examine Price and Bates, was to testify for the state. According to Dan T. Carter's account, Thomas Knight, in a private conference with Judge Horton, asked that Lynch be excused, since his testimony would be the same as Dr. Bridges's. Judge Horton agreed to excuse Lynch, only to be approached, shortly thereafter, by Lynch himself. Although he had been excused, Lynch said he wished to speak to Judge Horton privately. He wanted to tell the judge that he didn't wish to testify, not because his testimony duplicated Bridges's, but, rather, because it did not. Stunned, Judge Horton urged him to change his mind but Lynch held firm. "If I testified for those boys," he said, "I'd never be able to go back into Jackson County." Nearly forty years later, in 1967, Dr. Lynch was to deny ever making any of these comments to Judge Horton.[10]

Despite his misgivings and because he could not force Lynch to testify, having already excused him, Judge Horton decided to proceed with the trials. After a number of other witnesses, the state's attorney rested and Leibowitz began his defense.

In addition to putting the Scottsboro Boys themselves on the stand, Leibowitz called on various members of the Chattanooga community, from which Price and Bates hailed, to testify as to the women's characters and to the events on the train. Leibowitz was saving his star witness for the very last.

On Thursday, after Leibowitz had rested his case "with reservations," which meant that, if necessary, he could call further witnesses, he received a note from a messenger. After a brief consultation with Judge Horton and a short recess, Leibowitz called his final witness— Ruby Bates. As Leibowitz led her through her testimony, Bates said in a low voice that no assault had taken place either on herself or on Victoria Price that afternoon in 1931. Her conscience had bothered her, she said. She had gone to New York City to find someone to tell the truth to and had spoken with a New York minister, Dr. Harry Emerson Fosdick, who had urged her to return to Alabama and tell the truth. When asked why she had lied originally, Bates said she had been afraid and that Victoria Price had told her to tell the story of the assault because "she said we might have to lay out a sentence in jail" if she didn't.[11]

By this time, the courtroom was in an uproar. After admonishments from Judge Horton, the room quieted and Thomas Knight began his cross-examination. Bates's answers to his questions were feeble and, at times, contradictory. Aiming to give the impression that she had been bribed by the defense, Knight went over and over Bates's seemingly miraculous decision to tell the truth. Weakly she protested, but her denials and statements seemed only to turn the jury against her. "After she confessed," Haywood Patterson observed, "the people in Decatur went near screech-crazy. . . . one businessman said . . . 'Those girls and niggers all should be hung. Thirty cents worth of rope could cure the whole problem.' "[12] Judge Horton ordered National Guardsmen placed outside the courthouse in anticipation of trouble.

The next day the prosecution began its summation, led off by Morgan County Solicitor Wade Wright. Beginning quietly, Wright soon worked himself into a frenzy, shouting and waving his arms. "Show them," Wright cried to the jury, "show them that Alabama justice cannot be bought and sold with Jew money from New York."[13] At this, Leibowitz leapt up and called for a mistrial, but although Judge Horton admonished the prosecution, the trial continued.

After lengthy arguments by both Leibowitz and Knight, Judge Horton instructed the jury as to their duties. "We are not trying lawyers," he said. "We are not trying state lines. We are not trying whether the defendant is white or black."[14] The only question to consider, Judge Horton pointed out, was whether Haywood Patterson was guilty beyond a reasonable doubt.

The jury began deliberations just before 1:00 P.M. on Saturday and, at 10:00 A.M. on Sunday, announced that it had reached a decision. As the attorneys and Haywood Patterson sat waiting in the courtroom, they could hear laughter from the jury room. At 11:00 A.M., when the jurors were called in by Judge Horton, the twelve men filed in still laughing. Asked for their decision, the foreman read, "We find the defendant guilty as charged and fix the punishment at death in the electric chair."[15] As Haywood Patterson poignantly noted, "The sun came in the windows strong and made everything that was white look whiter, and me the one thing black, I guess, looked blacker."[16]

After the decision was read, Judge Horton postponed the remaining trials "until such time as the passions of the local citizens have subsided."[17] On June 22, 1933, the ILD lawyers requested that the judge schedule the remaining trials and hear a motion for a new trial for Haywood Patterson. When he announced the dates of the new trials, Judge Horton took the opportunity to issue a lengthy statement concerning the Scottsboro cases. After detailing all the evidence in the case of Haywood Patterson, Judge Horton concluded:

> History, sacred and profane, and the common experience of mankind teach us that women of the character shown in this case are prone for selfish reasons to make false accusations both of rape and of insult upon the slightest provocation, or even without provocation for ulterior purposes. These women are shown, by the great weight of the evidence, on this very day before leaving Chattanooga, to have falsely accused two negroes of insulting them, and of almost precipitating a fight between one of the white boys they were in company with and these two negroes. This tendency on the part of the women shows that they are predisposed to make false accusa-

tions upon any occasion whereby their selfish ends may be gained.

. . . .

The testimony of the prosecutrix in this case is not only uncorroborated, but it also bears on its face indications of improbability and is contradicted by other evidence, and in addition thereto the evidence greatly preponderates in favor of the defendant. It therefore becomes the duty of the Court under the law to grant the motion made in this case.

It is therefore ordered and adjudged by the Court that the motion be granted; that the verdict of the jury in this case and the judgment of the Court sentencing this defendant to death be set aside and that a new trial be and the same is hereby ordered.

JAMES E. HORTON
Circuit Judge[18]

Haywood Patterson would get a new trial; the judgment of the jury was set aside. Attorney General Thomas Knight vowed the retrial would commence as quickly as possible.

The ILD lawyers were overjoyed. Despite the bias of the juries in Alabama, justice had prevailed in this case. Judge Horton, on the other hand, was to suffer for his decision. The "Scottsboro Judge" was soundly defeated in his bid for reelection to his judgeship and was forced to retire into private practice. In that same election, Thomas Knight was elected Alabama's lieutenant governor.

As 1933 moved toward its close, the Scottsboro Boys found themselves back where they had started, facing a new set of trials. Yet there was hope. Twice, for Haywood Patterson at least, the death penalty had been imposed and twice justice had prevailed. It seemed, as Haywood Patterson himself said, "there could be white folks in the South with a right mind," after all.[19]

7
CALLAHAN'S COURT

J udge William Washington Callahan was seventy years old at the time the Scottsboro Boys appeared before him for their new trials. Unlike Judge Horton, Callahan didn't have the advantages of a college education; as a young man he had read law to pass the bar while working as a legal clerk in a law office. "This judge," noted Clarence Norris, "was a redneck from the word go. . . . It didn't matter to him if we were innocent or guilty, he was determined to send us to the electric chair."[1]

When Haywood Patterson's case came before Callahan in November 1933, the judge vowed that the trials would not be the circus that had been permitted by earlier judges. The people of Morgan County were "sober-minded," there was no need for the National Guard, and newsmen were to be limited in the court. These trials had dragged out far too long in Callahan's opinion. The best thing to do was to get them over quickly and be done with them. One way he went about doing so was to cut down on discussion and argument. Haywood Patterson observed that Callahan "let the state people talk all they wanted. But he shut up Liebowitz [sic] and the other International Labor Defense lawyers every minute. Callahan would sometimes object himself before the state did."[2]

Leibowitz began the trials with a motion for another change of venue. Morgan County citizens had been saturated with information regarding the whole Scottsboro case during the earlier trial before Judge Horton; their minds were made up regarding guilt or innocence. Callahan quickly dismissed the motion. Thomas Knight, again representing the state, had produced affidavits from Morgan County citizens who swore the trial would be fair. That was enough for Callahan.

Leibowitz next moved, again, for a change of venue and for negation of the indictments handed down by Jefferson County at the earlier trials. This time Leibowitz's reason was that there were no blacks on the jury rolls and there had not been any in 1931, the time of the original trials. Callahan overruled the motion. He was "not prepared to say that the officers . . . in selecting the jury list, have so administered the law as to violate the Constitution."[3]

To prove bias, Leibowitz called J. E. Moody, head of the jury commission, to the stand. Leibowitz asked Moody to read the names on the jury lists and the race of each man registered. Both the defense and prosecuting attorneys were surprised, however, when, in his recitation, Moody named at least ten black men. The next day, Leibowitz called a handwriting expert, John Vreeland Harding, to the stand. Harding stated that the books had been tampered with. After deliberation, however, Callahan denied the motion to quash the earlier indictments. He could not assume fraud had been committed, he said, because the jury board and the probate judge overseeing the rolls were officers of the law and it "would be a reflection on them."[4] Despite the fact that a crime had obviously been committed by the falsifying of the jury rolls, Callahan was determined to ignore it. These trials were going to be done *his* way, and they would be done quickly. "We're going to make speed beginning Monday," he told Leibowitz on November 24.[5] There would be no more shilly-shallying and clever motions.

Callahan kept his word. On Monday, when Leibowitz attempted to question jurors, Callahan told him to "hurry it along," and kept cutting short his examinations. This behavior continued during the trial itself. As the now familiar figures of Victoria Price, Dr. Bridges, Orville Gilley, and others took the stand, Judge Callahan repeatedly objected to or cut short Leibowitz's examination of the witnesses and overruled Leibowitz's objections to Knight's handling of the witnesses.

Unfortunately, Ruby Bates was not there to testify to the truth or falsity of the evidence presented. Frightened, she had returned to New York after the summer trials and refused to return. "Since I was in Decatur," she wrote to William Patterson in November, "almost every day now I get letters from the south calling me a 'nigger-

lover' and saying that I should be lynched too."[6] Leibowitz requested that the court allow him to question
Ruby Bates in New York, but on November 28 Bates
became ill and was hospitalized in New York, unable to
answer questions. When Leibowitz asked Callahan for a
delay so he could obtain Bates's testimony after she re-
covered, Callahan denied the request, telling him that
the trial would have to proceed without it. Callahan was
determined that the trial be over quickly regardless of
fairness or truth.

This sentiment was reflected in the judge's instructions
to the jury on November 30, 1933. Despite what the defense had said regarding the events on the train and the
character of Victoria Price, Callahan stated, "The law
would authorize conviction on the testimony of Victoria
Price alone, if, from that evidence, taken into consideration with all the other evidence in the case, both for the
State and for the defendant, convinced you beyond a
reasonable doubt that she had been ravished. The law
does not require corroboration."[7] In other words, the
jury could make their decision based solely on Victoria
Price's testimony. Callahan's statement confirmed the
obvious bias of the trial and the premise prevalent at
that time in Alabama that a white person's testimony
against a black person was enough to convict that black
person. This bias was supported when, after the judge
had instructed the jury as to the kinds of decisions and
sentences they could impose, Leibowitz approached the
bench and reminded Judge Callahan that he had omitted
mention of acquittal. Callahan, somewhat embarrassed,

was forced reluctantly to add that if the jury was "not satisfied beyond all reasonable doubt that the defendant is guilty as charged then he ought to be acquitted."[8] As the *Christian Century* newspaper noted, "It is inconceivable that a jury would not interpret the judge's original oversight and this perfunctory footnote as indicating that he did not consider acquittal as a serious possibility."[9]

The jury for Haywood Patterson's trial had barely left the courtroom to deliberate when Judge Callahan ordered jury selection to begin for the trial of Clarence Norris. Norris later wrote, "The jury looked like a lynch-mob; a bunch of tobacco-chewing, snuff-dipping, overalled crackers in muddy shoes."[10]

As Callahan began swearing in Norris's jury, Patterson's jury notified the court that a decision had been reached. The Norris jury was hastily removed from the courtroom and Haywood Patterson brought in looking, as a Decatur *Daily* reporter said, "like a caged animal about to lunge at a keeper who had mistreated him."[11] The court clerk, John Green, read the expected verdict: guilty with a sentence of death. Accordingly, the judge pronounced the sentence. Ordinarily, a judge announcing a sentence ends with "And may God have mercy on your soul." But not Judge Callahan. "When Callahan sentenced me to death for the third time," Patterson observed, "I noticed he left out the Lord. He didn't even want the Lord to have any mercy on me."[12]

The trial of Clarence Norris was a replay of Patterson's trial, with Leibowitz trying desperately to admit evidence and question witnesses but being overruled at every turn by Judge Callahan. "Liebowitz [sic] was a tiger though and gave it all he had," Norris later wrote.[13] By the time of Norris's trial, Leibowitz had obtained testimony from Ruby Bates, but the jury received the same instructions given to Patterson's jury: everything was to rest on Victoria Price's testimony. After twelve hours of deliberation, the jury returned with the verdict Callahan and the people of Alabama wanted. Clarence Norris was guilty and was, again, sentenced to death.

Although Callahan was prepared to begin the next trial, that of Charlie Weems, Leibowitz, depressed and discouraged, asked that the other trials be postponed until the decisions reached in Norris's and Patterson's trials could be appealed. "These trials," he said, "may be only an empty gesture after the courts have received them."[14] Callahan, appalled at the court costs so far incurred, granted the motion. Haywood Patterson and Clarence Norris were returned to death row in Kilby Prison; the remaining Scottsboro Boys were sent to the Birmingham jail to await the outcome of the appeals.

The convictions of Patterson and Norris had not gone unnoticed by the rest of the country. Protests and marches against the sentences were staged in Harlem and in other cities, but they did not rally the support seen in 1931. Despite local agreement that justice had been served, the Birmingham *Post* surprisingly condemned the trials also. "The record of this trial," noted the *Post* on December 2, 1933, "when it comes to review by the United States Supreme Court, will not be a favorable commentary on Alabama judicial procedure."

In February 1934, Judge Callahan denied a motion presented by ILD lawyers for Haywood Patterson to be granted a new trial. Leibowitz, with ILD attorneys Osmond K. Fraenkel and George W. Chamlee, began again the work of appealing the Patterson and Norris convictions to the Alabama Supreme Court.

On May 25, the Alabama Supreme Court sat to review the cases. Leibowitz once again argued the jury question. Osmond Fraenkel discussed Judge Callahan's conduct during the trials and the fact that he did not properly instruct the jury regarding acquittal.

Once again Thomas Knight appeared for the state. Patterson's case, he argued, should not even be considered because the defense lawyers had not filed the proper papers in time. Regarding Norris's case, Knight declared that jury selection and qualifications were not the province of the Alabama Supreme Court, but rather came under the authority of the jury commissions. "If this court," said Knight, "with no evidence showing that Negroes were excluded, holds that systematic exclusion of Negroes took place, then the court is constituting itself the jury commission of every court in Alabama."[15]

Knight's reasoning dominated the decision of the court. On Thursday, June 28, the Alabama Supreme Court denied the appeals of both Norris and Patterson. They upheld Knight's declaration that, in Patterson's case, the documents necessary had not been filed in the proper amount of time and that, in both cases, blacks were not "excluded" from the jury rolls. The jury commission had, rather, "selected" certain jurors as opposed to others. As to Judge Callahan's conduct, the court admitted he had "on one or two occasions manifested slight impatience," but the trials themselves were speedy and fair.[16]

Since Patterson's case had been set aside because of the ruling that the proper papers had not been filed in time, it could not be appealed to the United States Supreme Court with Norris's, for technically his case had never been appealed to the state courts. On July 9, however, George Chamlee filed for a rehearing for Patterson's case by the Alabama Supreme Court. This, in effect, acted as a stay of execution for Patterson. At the same time, ILD lawyers began the steps to appeal Norris's case to the United States Supreme Court. In the meantime, however, the ILD's reputation was being harmed through the machinations of Victoria Price. Documents in the files of the ILD and the American Scottsboro Committee attest that Price offered to change her story for the right price and that ILD officials had taken her up on the offer.

In June of 1934, ILD official J. T. Pearson told the ILD officials in New York that Victoria Price had said to him that she would change her story for the right amount of money. Joseph Brodsky asked Samuel Schriftman, a New York attorney, to handle the negotiations and, after some discussion, on October 1, 1934, Schriftman agreed to meet with Price. Schriftman and another acquaintance of Brodsky's, Sol Kone, flew to Cincinnati and chartered a plane to Nashville, carrying $1,500 in cash for Victoria Price. They were to meet her in a hotel in Nashville where she would sign an affidavit stating that her testimony had been false. J. T. Pearson was to drive her to Nashville for the meeting.

In the meantime, Price had decided to double-cross the ILD and had notified Huntsville, Alabama, police of the deal. As a result, Pearson, Schriftman, and Kone were all arrested for attempting to bribe a witness.

When Leibowitz heard of the ILD's actions, he was furious. The ILD had "assassinated the Scottsboro boys with that sort of business," he said. It was better for the ILD to get out of the cases completely, he felt, since they had sullied them.

As 1934 drew to a close, the same sort of clash that had marred the defense of the Scottsboro Boys earlier seemed to be reoccurring. Leibowitz was determined to defend the Scottsboro Boys without the ILD, and the ILD was determined to maintain its role in the cases. Once again the parents of the Scottsboro Boys were enlisted by each side to sway the nine men and boys. As Clarence Norris said, "So, there we were, stuck in the middle again."[17]

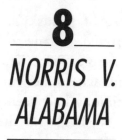

8
NORRIS V. ALABAMA

During the fall of 1934, the parade of parents at Kilby Prison pulled the Scottsboro Boys first in one direction, then another. At one point, at the urging of their mothers and ILD attorney Benjamin Davis, Norris and Patterson each signed an affidavit stating, "I want my present appeal in the United States Supreme Court to be handled exclusively by the International Labor Defense."[1] The next week, Leibowitz's aide was able to obtain a statement saying that the two would stick by Leibowitz, and explaining that the "Communists have been sending their agents here and have our minds bewildered."[2]

Earlier in October, Leibowitz had met with the New York Interdenominational Association of Preachers and had gained their support. They had formed an American Scottsboro Committee to aid in the defense of the Scottsboro Boys, but although they had no ties with the ILD, they were unable to gain support for their cause in the South. The continued presence of Leibowitz and his past associations with the ILD prevented the Scottsboro Boys from getting any support from citizens in Alabama.

Amid this tug-of-war, Haywood Patterson still had faith in the ILD, although Norris favored Leibowitz. Accordingly, early in 1935, Leibowitz met with the ILD attorneys and reached an agreement. Norris would be represented by Leibowitz and Chamlee (who had, like Leibowitz, disavowed any ties with the ILD), and Osmond Fraenkel and Walter Pollak of the ILD would defend Patterson. The agreement was vital; the United States Supreme Court had ruled on January 7, 1935, that it would review the convictions of Patterson and Norris.

On February 15, 1935, a nervous Samuel Leibowitz began his first presentation before the Supreme Court in *Norris v. Alabama*. Leibowitz argued that blacks had been systematically excluded from the Jackson County jury rolls and that the names of those blacks who had been listed on the rolls were forged. Leibowitz presented the jury rolls for examination, explaining how the forgeries took place.

Once again Thomas G. Knight, Jr., spoke for the state of Alabama. As in the Callahan trials and before the Alabama Supreme Court, he argued that blacks were not "excluded"; rather, they merely were not "selected." Regarding the issue of forgery, Knight stated he could not "tell . . . whether or not those names were forged. I simply take the position that I do not know."[3]

Walter Pollak argued Haywood Patterson's case. The

Alabama Supreme Court had ruled that the United States Supreme Court had no jurisdiction over Patterson's case because a bill of exception had not been filed in the proper amount of time by Patterson's attorneys. Pollak argued regarding the obvious unfairness of the situation. Because of a mere technicality, one defendant, Norris, might gain a new trial, while the other, Patterson, might be sent to his death. Thomas Knight argued his best for upholding the absolute letter of the law, but the injustice of the situation was quite evident. The Supreme Court ruled, "At least the state court should have an opportunity to examine its powers in the light of the situation which has now developed."[4] The Supreme Court then sent Patterson's case back to the Alabama Supreme Court.

In deciding *Norris v. Alabama*, the Court considered the constitutional issue of the right of all citizens to equal protection under the law as guaranteed by the Fourteenth Amendment. Leibowitz argued that the state of Alabama had violated this principle by preventing blacks from serving on juries. The Court ruled:

> The testimony, as the State Court said, tended to show that "in a long number of years no Negro had been called for jury service in that county." It appeared that no Negro had been called for jury service on any grand or petit jury in that county within the living memory of witnesses who had lived there all their lives. Testimony to that effect was given by men whose ages ran from 50 to 76 years. Their testimony was un-

contradicted. It was supported by the testimony of officials.

. . . .

That testimony in itself made out a prima facie [apparent] case of the denial of equal protection which the Constitution guarantees.[5]

The Supreme Court then ruled on whether the names of blacks on the Jackson County jury rolls for 1930–1931 were forgeries. Callahan had ruled that the names had been properly added and were not forgeries. The Supreme Court, after examining the evidence, ruled:

We think that the evidence did not justify that opinion. The Supreme Court of the State did not sustain it. The court observed that the charge that the names of Negroes were fraudulently placed on the roll did not involve any member of the jury board and that the charge "was, by implication, at least, laid at the door of the clerk of the board."[6]

The Court also examined the issue of whether the trial should have been held in Morgan County or elsewhere. In writing the majority opinion, Chief Justice Charles Evans Hughes quoted the jury commissioner of Morgan County, whose statement Knight had produced to *support* holding the trials there. "I do not know," the jury commissioner had stated, "of any Negro in Morgan County over twenty-one and under sixty-five who is generally reputed to be honest and intelligent and who is esteemed in the community for his integrity, good character and sound judgement, who is not an habitual drunkard, who isn't afflicted with a permanent disease or physical weakness which would render him unfit to discharge the duties of a juror and who can read English and who has never been convicted of a crime involving moral turpitude."

The Supreme Court, Justice Hughes stated, just could not believe this:

> In the light of the testimony given by the defendant's witnesses, we find it impossible to accept such a sweeping characterization of the lack of qualifications of Negroes in Morgan County. It is so sweeping and so contrary to the evidence, as to the many qualified Negroes, that it destroys the intended effect of the commissioner's testimony.

The Court, Justice Hughes read, ruled, "The judgment must be reversed and the cause remanded for further proceedings not inconsistent with this opinion. It is so ordered."[7] To deprive blacks of the opportunity to serve on juries was a violation of the Fourteenth Amendment, and to refuse Clarence Norris a trial before his peers, black and white, deprived him of his right to equal protection under the law. Norris and Patterson were to be given new trials.

The Communist Party celebrated the decisions as proof of the effectiveness of the ILD defense. Leibowitz, however, saw them as a "triumph for American justice and . . . an answer to all those subversive elements who seek to engender hatred against our form of government."[8] The two groups were still at odds.

In Alabama, the reactions to *Norris v. Alabama* were anger and stunned disbelief. How dare the Supreme Court dictate what Alabama and its citizens must do? The Montgomery *Advertiser* of April 3, 1935, derisively asked, "If negroes had served on Jackson County court justice every year for 29 years before the 'Scottsboro' infants came into court in their diapers and shaking their baby rattles, but for some reason—any reason—had not been drawn to serve on the jury that tried the infants aforesaid, would the . . . Supreme Court . . . have solemnly averred that justice had been outraged?"

Despite the scorn and anger of Alabama's citizens, the highest court in the land had ruled. Governor Bibb Graves sent a letter to all circuit judges and lawyers in Alabama on April 5, 1935, telling them that the ruling of the Supreme Court must be obeyed. Blacks must be placed on the jury rolls: "This decision means that we must put the names of Negroes in jury boxes in every county in the State."[9]

Sensing some hope in Graves's admonitions to the Alabama legal system, Leibowitz wrote to Governor Graves on April 30, 1935, asking him either to have the cases of the Scottsboro Boys dropped or to turn them over to an impartial fact-finding committee for study. The trials had dragged on for four years, Leibowitz pointed out, costing the state a great deal of money. In view of the background of Victoria Price, this misery should not be allowed to continue.

Graves chose not to reply to Leibowitz's letter, and on May 1, 1935, Victoria Price swore out new warrants against the Scottsboro Boys. On November 13 of that same year, the grand jury at Scottsboro issued new indictments against all the Scottsboro Boys, including Roy Wright and Eugene Williams, whose cases had earlier been transferred to juvenile court. As the *New York Times* reported on April 7, it was the "inflexible if misguided conviction of many Alabamians . . . that a fresh start be made now in the business of getting the accused men to the electric chair."

Clarence Norris later reflected the feelings of all the Scottsboro Boys when he plaintively wrote, "We had been in jail for over four years, shuttling back and forth between Decatur, Birmingham, and Montgomery, from cell to cell and trial to trial. I wondered how much longer the State of Alabama would spend its money to prosecute nine innocent boys in order to send them to their deaths."[10]

9
BACK TO DECATUR

Throughout 1935, controversy again erupted as to who would represent the Scottsboro Boys in their new trials. The ILD, realizing that to garner more public support it could not remain as inflexible as it had been in the past, approached a number of other groups to form a defense coalition. On December 19, 1935, the NAACP, the ILD, the ACLU, the League for Industrial Democracy (LID), and the Methodist Federation for Social Service joined together to create the Scottsboro Defense Committee (SDC). Because it represented a variety of beliefs, the SDC hoped to sway some Alabamians to support its efforts to free the Scottsboro Boys. Since it was not just an ILD effort, Samuel Leibowitz agreed to cooperate with the coalition, and the earlier American Scottsboro Committee was dissolved.

But Leibowitz's cooperation was, to some extent, a liability in the SDC's attempts to gain local support in Alabama. Because of his persistence in defending the Scottsboro Boys and because he was from New York

and Jewish, Alabamians resented his continuing participation in the case, as well as the continuing presence of
the ILD. To mollify the Alabamians, the SDC promised
that Leibowitz would remain somewhat in the background at the new trials.

Despite weak local support, the SDC lawyers once
again set about the task of preparing for the new trials.
As in the 1934 trials, the plan was to ask for a change
of venue, for if the Scottsboro Boys were to appear
again before Judge Callahan, their chances for acquittal
would be nearly nonexistent. Huntsville, Alabama, de-
tective John A. Hackworth was hired to sample local
feelings. Hackworth, expectedly, found "great bitterness
and hostility ... expressed toward the defendants and
their attorneys," along with some talk of lynching the
Scottsboro Boys.[1]

On January 6, 1936, the Scottsboro Boys were once
again arraigned in Judge Callahan's court. Osmond
Fraenkel, speaking for the defense, then asked for a
change in venue—not to another Alabama court district,
but to the nearest federal district court. Judge Callahan
was incensed by the implication that the defendants
could not get a fair trail in an Alabama court. In re-
jecting the motion, Callahan angrily called it "irrelevant,
and ... improper," saying, "There isn't a solitary decision of the Supreme Court of the United States that has
held that you can have a case removed ... unless and
until it is shown by a petition that the state has passed
some law that infringes these [defendants'] rights."[2]
With that, Callahan set the trials to begin on Janu-

ary 20, starting, for a fourth time, with Haywood Patterson.

"Up north," Haywood Patterson wrote, "and around the country people were speaking about us. Even Ruby Bates, she traveled around the country telling of the frame-up."[3] Once again public fervor both for and against the Scottsboro Boys was aroused. But people were tiring of the subject, and the massive funds the earlier trials had generated for their defense were not forthcoming from the public in this set of trials.

In accordance with the Supreme Court ruling and Governor Graves's orders, out of the hundred people called for jury duty for the new trials, twelve were black. Fearful and hesitant over being questioned about serving on the jury, the twelve black men were not even permitted to sit in the jury box during pretrial examination. They were ordered by Judge Callahan to sit in the Negro section of the courtroom. Seven of the twelve asked permission to be excused from jury duty for personal reasons, permission quickly granted by Judge Callahan. The remaining five were speedily rejected by the state prosecutor during questioning. Obviously relieved, they quickly left the courthouse. Had they served, their lives and those of their families would have been in danger.

On January 21, 1935, Patterson's fourth trial got under way with Thomas Knight once again leading the prosecution. Again Victoria Price took the stand and reiterated her now familiar story. Once again, Judge Callahan prohibited the defense lawyers, consisting of

Clarence Watts, Samuel Leibowitz, and George Chalmers, from delving into her seamy background.

In earlier trials, Price's testimony had been supported by that of Orville Gilley, the white man who had remained on the train after the fight between the two groups, black and white. Now this was impossible. Only the week before the trials began, Gilley had been convicted in the state of Tennessee for assaulting and robbing two women and was imprisoned there. To replace Gilley, Knight produced Obie Golden, a guard at Kilby Prison. In 1934, Golden testified, Patterson had confessed to him, saying, "I am guilty of that crime. Also Clarence Norris and also those other seven up there in Birmingham Jail."[4]

Leibowitz cross-examined Golden, pressing him to tell why, in addition to neither telling the warden of this "confession" nor writing it down, he had waited nearly a year and a half to report it. Golden had no answer. Patterson later said, "He was a liar. I told the court so."[5]

Once again earning his nickname, Speed Callahan, the judge pushed to have the trial over as quickly as possible. As in the previous trials, he abruptly cut short questioning by the defense and inserted his own objections to testimony and questioning. On January 23, only two days after the trial had commenced, the defense rested its case and summations began.

Melvin Hutson, the Morgan County solicitor, gave the summation for the prosecution. Hutson, who had a flair for the dramatic, alternately shouted at and cajoled the jury, setting Victoria Price up as a representative of all defenseless southern women. If the jury did not find Patterson guilty, he said, Alabama women would have "to buckle six-shooters about their middles" to protect themselves. "Don't go out and quibble over the evidence. Say to yourselves, 'We're tired of this job' and put it behind you. Get it done quick and protect the fair womanhood of this great State."[6]

In contrast, Clarence Watts spoke quietly for the defense, pointing out that the testimonies of Victoria Price and other prosecution witnesses were contradicted by the physical facts in the case. He urged the jury to consider the case fairly, adding, "It takes courage to do the right thing in the face of public clamor for the wrong thing."[7]

In his instructions to the jury, Judge Callahan essentially repeated those of the previous trials, adding one new feature. This time he also told the jurors that they might find Patterson guilty of conspiracy to the charge of assault. Patterson's defense attorneys loudly and in vain protested that conspiracy was not even one of the charges for which Patterson had been indicted. Callahan refused to retract his words, however. In the *New York Times*, reporter Carleton Beals pointed out that both Callahan's words and demeanor could only lead the jury to one verdict: guilty. "Judge Callahan said that if such and such things were true, in a tone implying they probably were, then the defendant was a 'rapist' and should be convicted [and] . . . he glared over at the defendant in fury, his lips drawn back in a snarl, and he rolled out the word 'r-r-rapist' in a horrendous tone."[8]

As expected, the jury found Haywood Patterson guilty of the charges against him, but there was one surprise. When the sentence was announced, instead of imposing the death penalty, the jury fixed his sentence at seventy-five years in prison. Knight and Hutson were shocked by the sentence; Callahan was clearly angry. The judge asked the foreman if the jury had thoroughly considered the sentence. The foreman timidly assured him they had.

The defense lawyers viewed the sentence as a sort of victory; obviously inroads were being made on Alabama bias. But, Haywood Patterson said, "it was no victory for me. . . . I felt bad. I knew I was going to be driven to a slow death. . . . These people didn't know what the Alabama prisons were like. I already had a five-year taste of it. It was living death."[9]

On January 24, the trial of Clarence Norris was to begin, but Leibowitz, Watts, and Chalmers requested a postponement because Dr. Bridges, a key witness for both sides, was ill. After some haggling, Judge Callahan granted a postponement until Dr. Bridges was well enough to testify. The Scottsboro Boys were loaded into cars to be driven back to the Birmingham jail to await the new trials.

The sentence of seventy-five years seemed to the SDC and the defense lawyers to be a sign that, perhaps, there might be hope for the Scottsboro Boys in the Alabama court system after all. But any slim hope raised by the sentence was dashed the same day on the road to the Birmingham jail. The Alabama authorities had gotten three cars to take the Scottsboro Boys to the Birmingham jail and had put three prisoners in each car. Ozie Powell, Clarence Norris, and Roy Wright were traveling in the middle car with Morgan County Sheriff J. Street Sandlin and his deputy, Edgar Blalock.

According to Norris: "Blaylock [sic] started in cussing our 'Communist, Jew, Northern lawyer.' . . . Ozie Powell told him, 'I wouldn't give up the help I have for no damn Southern lawyer that I've seen."[10] At that, Blalock turned in his seat and slapped Powell across the face. Suddenly, Powell leaned forward and slashed the deputy with a knife he had managed to obtain.

"Our car," Norris said, "was zigzagging across the highway because the sheriff had pulled his gun and was trying to shoot into the backseat and drive too." The sheriff finally was able to pull the car over, and the third car in the procession quickly pulled in behind him. Both sheriff and deputy jumped from the car, and as a patrolman from the third car ran up asking what was happening, Sheriff Sandlin said, " 'One of the black bastards cut the deputy. I am going to get rid of [them] right now!' He fired into the car and shot Ozie."[11]

Thomas Knight, who had been following, quickly loaded the deputy into his car and had him driven to the nearest hospital. Ozie Powell, shot in the head and critically injured, was left handcuffed to Norris and Wright while all three were driven to the Birmingham jail. Only after the others were safely locked up was Powell taken to a hospital, where doctors only gave him a fifty-fifty chance of living. Powell did survive, but as Clarence Norris commented, "He was never the same as he was, not as bright or intelligent."[12]

Leibowitz, who had been on his way back to New York, immediately turned his car around and headed for Birmingham. When he questioned Norris and Wright the next day, they told him what had happened, but by that time Sheriff Sandlin was saying there had been no conversation between the deputy and the prisoners at all and that the whole incident had been an unprovoked attack that was part of an escape attempt. Chattanooga *News* editor George Fort Milton reported to Norman Thomas of the NAACP that the entire affair had "re-intensified all of the old feelings, and has made confusion even worse confounded than before."[13]

While the citizens of Alabama self-righteously condemned the Scottsboro Boys and charged Ozie Powell with assault and attempted murder, the rest of the country was skeptical. After all the publicity surrounding the Scottsboro cases, the rest of the United States had little faith in the reporting of the incident by the Alabama press. Public attitudes in Alabama subtly shifted. While most citizens didn't wish to see the Scottsboro Boys go free, the hostility and anger with which they had demanded the death penalty had cooled off. Now the overwhelming desire was to see an end to the entire business.

With this feeling in the air, Leibowitz saw a chance to reach a compromise with the state. At a meeting with

Thomas Knight, who had been elected lieutenant governor, and Attorney General A. A. Carmichael, it was agreed that, as historian Dan Carter writes, "Haywood Patterson's appeal would be withdrawn and Ozie Powell would be tried only for assault on Deputy Blalock. Charlie Weems, Andy Wright, and Clarence Norris would plead guilty to some form of assault and would receive sentences of less than five years. Eventually Haywood Patterson would be released so that his term in prison should not be more than [the others']."[14] However, when Judge Callahan was approached regarding this compromise, he angrily refused to accept it. There was no way the Scottsboro Boys were going to get off so easily. On June 14, the Alabama Supreme Court upheld the conviction of Haywood Patterson, and only a week or two later, Thomas Knight suddenly died.

With Knight dead and Callahan adamantly against a compromise, there was no alternative but for Samuel Leibowitz and the SDC lawyers to begin preparation for the trials of Clarence Norris and the other Scottsboro Boys. Judge Callahan scheduled these for the summer of 1937; Alabama justice ground inexorably on.

10
FINAL TRIALS AND TRIBULATIONS

Summer in Alabama is slow and steamy. At Clarence Norris's final trial, beginning on July 12, 1937, the heat lay like an unwanted blanket over the baking countryside. Defense counsel Clarence Watts, Norris relates, collapsed. Alone and mopping his brow, Leibowitz carried on with the pretrial motions and jury selection. The prosecution was handled by Thomas Lawson, a candidate for attorney general in the upcoming election.

As before, the trial opened with the testimony of Victoria Price, who, according to Norris, "took the stand and told her tired old lies."[1] Once again, on cross-examination, she countered the defense's questions with "I don't know" and "I can't remember." Dr. Bridges had died in March of 1936, but Judge Callahan permitted Leibowitz to read his previous testimony into the record, with no objection from Thomas Lawson.

Unlike in earlier trials, Leibowitz was permitted to

call witnesses to testify to Victoria Price's character. Richard S. Watson, who had been deputy sheriff in Huntsville, Alabama, testified, "I would not believe her under oath," and Sol Wallace, a Madison County deputy sheriff, confirmed this opinion, saying, "I would not believe anything she said."[2] Although this testimony and that of Emma Bates, Ruby Bates's mother, was damning, the jury chose to ignore it. On July 15, 1937, after two and one-half hours of deliberation, the jury found Clarence Norris guilty and sentenced him to death.

The sentence was a blow to both Leibowitz and Watts, although it could be explained by the incident on the road to the Birmingham jail. Norris had been in the same car as Powell; that was enough to implicate him in the knifing of the deputy sheriff in the minds of the jurors. After Judge Callahan announced that the trial of Andy Wright would then commence, Clarence Watts shakily arose and asked for a delay; he was too ill from the heat to continue. The pressure of the trial and the hostility Watts had met with from his Huntsville friends who felt he was betraying Alabama by defending the Scottsboro Boys were too much for him. Judge Callahan, seeing Watts's condition, recessed the court for a week to allow Watts to recover.

As with Norris's trial, Andy Wright's trial was swift and final. Although found guilty, he was sentenced to ninety-five years in prison, not to death. Charlie Weems's trial was next.

Faced, as always, with the obstructing admonitions from Judge Callahan, frustrated by the years of injustice, Leibowitz vented his anger in his summation of the case against Charlie Weems. "I'm sick and tired," he shouted, "of this sanctimonius hypocrisy. It isn't Charlie Weems on trial in this case, it's a Jew lawyer and New York State put on trial here by the inflammatory remarks of Mr. Bailey [of the prosecution]." People in Alabama were liars, Leibowitz said. All the jurors over the years whom he had questioned had righteously sworn up and down that they had no prejudice against blacks. But walk out on the streets, Leibowitz challenged, and all the whites questioned damned the blacks to prison. If the state asked for a particular sentence against a black man, the state got it. *That* was how justice in Alabama worked.[3]

During this tirade, prosecuting attorney Thomas Lawson became so infuriated that he left the courtroom. Judge Callahan, anger written across his face, paced back and forth behind the bench, unable—because of the rules governing summations—to stop Leibowitz's flow of words. Despite the emotion and strength of Leibowitz's arguments, after nearly two and one-half hours of deliberation the jury returned a verdict of guilty. Charlie Weems was sentenced to seventy-five years in prison. Immediately afterward, Ozie Powell was brought into the courtroom for his trial.

From this point on, however, the script changed. Whether these changes were due to the previous agreement that had been worked out with Thomas Knight or to Leibowitz's outburst, or the exhaustion the trials had engendered in everyone over the years, hope suddenly reared its head. Lawson announced that the state had agreed to drop the assault charges against Powell and charge him only for attacking Deputy Blalock. After muttered consultation with Samuel Leibowitz, Ozie Powell pleaded guilty to attacking the deputy and Judge Callahan set his sentence at twenty years. Leibowitz argued that the six years Powell had already spent in prison should be subtracted from this, but Callahan said only if it "had not been that the State had dropped the other charge of rape against him, I would have given him fifteen years."[4]

After Powell's sentencing, Thomas Lawson approached the bench and began a whispered conference with Judge Callahan and Leibowitz. Suddenly Leibowitz walked quickly out of the courtroom and across the street to the county jail. Telling Olen Montgomery, Roy Wright, Willie Roberson, and Eugene Williams to follow him, he led them out of the jail and put them into two waiting cars. Getting in with them, Leibowitz headed for New York City. Suddenly, almost before anyone realized it, four of the Scottsboro Boys were free.

Speculation about the "deal" was the talk of Alabama. According to Clarence Norris, "The attorney general's office issued a statement that the five left behind were clearly guilty but the four that were freed had been the victims of mistaken identity."[5]

The Scottsboro Boys left in prison in Alabama felt betrayed. Clarence Norris called it "the saddest day of my life."[6] How, they all asked, could four be guilty and five, including Powell, be innocent? "The worst thing was," said Norris, "nobody explained nothing to the rest of us. Not one word from Leibowitz or anybody else."[7] As Haywood Patterson commented, "For the boys *let off* it was a victory. For those of us *dealt off* it was something else."[8]

Newspapers around the country echoed the perplexity of the remaining four Scottsboro Boys. The Richmond, Virginia, *Times-Dispatch* pointed out that the deal "serves as a virtual clincher to the argument that all nine of the Negroes are innocent."[9] Different versions of the deal were quickly circulated from various quarters. Even SDC chairman Allan Chalmers said, "I still cannot make out what he [Leibowitz] did nor did not do in Alabama in a deal."[10]

For the remaining Scottsboro Boys, the future looked hopeless. On October 26, 1937, the United States Supreme Court refused to review Haywood Patterson's and Clarence Norris's convictions and sentences. The SDC knew that Alabama's case against Charlie Weems and Andy Wright was the same as that against Patterson and Norris, so it did not appeal them beyond the Alabama Supreme Court. Rather, it went to Governor Bibb Graves on the matter.

On November 11, 1937, Chalmers wrote to Governor Graves asking if he might be permitted to discuss the Scottsboro matter with him. Forney Johnston of the SDC and two friends added a petition to Chalmers's letter asking that the governor use his powers to pardon the remaining Scottsboro Boys. The governor agreed to meet with Chalmers and other SDC members on December 21, 1937.

At the conference, after some discussion, Governor Graves stated, "I cannot make any promises which would look like a deal. I have already stated my feeling that the position of the State is untenable with half out and half in on the same charges and evidence. My mind is clear on the action required to remedy this impossible position. When the cases come before me I intend to act promptly. I cannot be any clearer than that, can I?"[11]

The agreement reached was that, after the cases of Norris, Weems, Wright, and Patterson went through the appeals process of the Alabama Supreme Court, the Pardoning Board, which advised Governor Graves, would meet and the four would be pardoned. They were to be paroled in October of 1938 and be on parole for six months thereafter.

On June 16, 1938, the Alabama Supreme Court upheld the convictions of the four Scottsboro Boys and set the date of Clarence Norris's execution for August 19, 1938. As promised, Governor Graves then commuted Norris's sentence to life imprisonment. Chalmers and the SDC then waited for the rest of the agreement to be completed, freeing the remaining Scottsboro Boys. Word passed to Chalmers that all but Ozie Powell would be released on October 31, 1938, and he and Morris Shapiro made arrangements to get the four men safely out of Alabama. But on October 29, Chalmers suddenly received a telegram from Governor Graves stating:

"Please defer Monday's engagement until further notice. Am not ready to act. Please acknowledge receipt."[12] Chalmers, who was in New York City, quickly phoned a friend in Alabama, Grover Hall, who promised to see what was up.

According to Hall, who had spoken with Graves, the governor was now determined not to parole the Scottsboro defendants. On October 29, Hall said, the governor had interviewed the four men and had been dismayed by their attitudes. Understandably bitter and unrepentant, the four, according to Clarence Norris, had been "sassy to him," and a knife had been found on Haywood Patterson. In his letter to Chalmers, Grover Hall said that the governor had stated: "They will humiliate you, Grover, they will humiliate Dr. Chalmers and Mr. Shapiro, they will humiliate Comer and Johnston and all other decent sponsors. They are anti-social, they are bestial, and they are unbelievably stupid and I do not believe they can be rehabilitated in freedom."[13]

Chalmers was able to persuade Governor Graves to put off announcing his decision, hoping to change his mind. But in the meantime, the five Scottsboro Boys remained in prison. Andy Wright, Charlie Weems, and Clarence Norris remained at Kilby Prison with Ozie Powell. Haywood Patterson was transferred to Atmore Prison Farm because the warden of Kilby Prison felt he was a troublemaker. Atmore was known as the worst prison in the South. As Haywood Patterson said, "The people all over the state of Alabama, they call that place *Murderers' Home*."[14]

Governor Graves had no intention of changing his mind. James Edward Chappell, the publisher and editor of the Birmingham *Age Herald*, told Chalmers that Graves had gotten "cold feet." It was not politically expedient for him to pardon the Scottsboro Boys; if he did so, he would not be reelected. Despite the fact that on December 24, 1938, Chalmers made public all his correspondence with the governor to try to force his hand, Graves remained firm. The Scottsboro Boys would stay in jail.

11
THE
AFTERMATH

With Governor Bibb Graves's refusal to consider parole for Clarence Norris, Andy Wright, Haywood Patterson, and Charlie Weems (Powell, having been convicted of assault, was in a different position), and with the other four Scottsboro Boys free in New York City, the Scottsboro cases faded from public attention. The nation was turning from its own troubles to those of Europe and the threat of Adolf Hitler's growing influence in Germany. Yet, quietly, and on his own for the most part, Allan Chalmers continued the battle to free the remaining Scottsboro Boys.

Helped by Grover Hall until Hall's death in 1941, Chalmers kept up a campaign of letter-writing and appeals to politicians and authorities in Alabama. In these efforts, the four freed defendants—Roy Wright, Olen Montgomery, Willie Roberson, and Eugene Williams—were more of a liability than an asset. Upon their arrival in New York City, the four had been taken in hand by a black minister from Brooklyn, Thomas C. Harten. He convinced them that they had been used by the SDC and by Samuel Leibowitz. Harten told the four that both the organization and Leibowitz had made a fortune from their cases. The four confronted Leibowitz and told him that they were through with him; they were going to make their own money and become rich. They marched out of Leibowitz's office without allowing him a chance even to speak. On August 15, 1937, Harten, who was now their manager, announced that the four were going onstage and booked them into Harlem's Apollo Theatre as "the symbol of a struggle for enlightenment and human brotherhood which will go on and on until it is won."[1]

Expecting to be rolling in money after their various appearances, the four Scottsboro Boys were soon disgusted and disillusioned. They were paid fairly, but Harten deducted a substantial fee from their salaries, and the four had to pay for new clothes and other expenses, leaving them little. All too soon, Montgomery, Wright, Roberson, and Williams were back on the doorstep of the SDC, asking for help. Having literally grown up in prison, it was difficult for the four to adjust to the outside world. They were untrained in all but the most menial jobs and nearly illiterate; there was little available for them to do. Ignoring their past complaints, the SDC set about finding them jobs and helping them become accustomed to their new lives. Eventually, Eugene Williams, Roy Wright, and Willie Roberson settled down and married, but, even then, there were problems.

In 1959, after stabbing his wife to death in a jealous rage, Roy Wright committed suicide.

Olen Montgomery had the most difficulty adjusting to life outside of prison. Nearly blind and a heavy drinker, Montgomery spent the rest of his life in and out of scrapes with the law on minor charges, relying on the SDC and, later, on the NAACP for handouts and help when he was in trouble. After traveling to a number of cities, he finally returned to Monroe, Georgia, where he had been born, and settled there.

Montgomery's numerous encounters with the law for drunkenness and fighting irritated Allan Chalmers, for they detracted from his efforts to get the remaining men out of prison. At the same time, Montgomery's situation saddened him. Chalmers said, "I have the feeling that even though we get the rest of them out, they are probably already too ruined by this experience . . . to adjust . . . to life in this already maladjusted world."[2]

Chalmers was determined to free the remaining Scottsboro Boys, however, and there did appear to be some hope. In August of 1939, the Alabama legislature enacted legislation creating a three-man Pardons and Paroles Board, removing those powers from the office of the governor. The new board said that they were favorably disposed to reviewing the Scottsboro cases. Grover Hall reported to Chalmers that things looked promising. However, Hall and Chalmers again failed to take into account Alabama politics and inbred bias, both of which came together in ex-Senator Thomas J. Heflin. When he heard that parole was being considered for the remaining Scottsboro Boys, Heflin vowed to stop it. He announced that he would appear before the Pardons and Paroles Board and speak against it. At his appearance before the board, Heflin railed against the idea, calling the Scottsboro Boys "vile despoilers of our precious white women."[3] The board voted against parole.

Meanwhile Norris, Weems, Patterson, Wright, and Powell were suffering in the Alabama prison system, one of the worst in the country at that time. Kilby Prison had a population of about five thousand inmates and was riddled with brutality and deprivation. Andy Wright wrote that the daily schedule consisted of being routed out "in the mornings at 4 o'clock and eat at 4:45 and don't eat dinner until 1:00 P.M. . . . and the worst part of it [is] we don't haff enough to eat."[4] All of them reported being brutalized by the guards and other inmates. Despite these conditions, however, they all clung to the hope of someday being released.

At Atmore Prison Farm Haywood Patterson suffered from the same degradations. Something of an opportunist, however, Patterson lost no chance to try to exploit his situation, attempting to get money from Chalmers and from groups that supported the release of the Scottsboro Boys. While Chalmers was working on their parole, Patterson knew he wanted them to stay out of trouble. Patterson, therefore, would threaten "bad trouble" or suicide if Chalmers didn't send him spending money.

Finally, in November of 1943, after five years of negotiating, the Alabama Pardons and Paroles Board released Charlie Weems. In January of 1944, Clarence Norris and Andy Wright were also paroled but, unlike Weems, were forbidden to leave the state. Instead, the parole officers found them back-breaking jobs at a lumber company, where they were forced to live together in a small room with only one bed. Faced with conditions no different from those in prison, Norris and Wright fled the state, violating their parole. Chalmers still hoped to gain freedom for Patterson, but the flight of Norris and Wright damned his efforts. After speaking with the two, and obtaining an agreement from the Pardons and Paroles Board that they would not be prosecuted or jailed if they returned, Chalmers was able to persuade them to return to Alabama. But when both returned, they were immediately sent back to prison, despite the agreement.

In 1944, faced with a growing lack of interest and funds, the SDC disbanded and Chalmers continued alone. After two more years, Norris was given another parole, as was Ozie Powell, who had been convicted only on the charge of assaulting Deputy Blalock. Norris knew what parole in Alabama was like and, at the first opportunity, fled to New York City, where he settled down, refusing to return.

Haywood Patterson knew his own odds for parole were nearly nonexistent. Described as "sullen, vicious and incorrigible" by the Pardons and Paroles Board, he had virtually no chance of release.[5] Thus, Patterson seized his opportunity in the summer of 1948 and escaped from Atmore Prison Farm with another inmate.

After making his way to the home of his sister in Detroit, Michigan, he remained in hiding for two years. In 1950 he was captured by the Federal Bureau of Investigation, but Michigan Governor G. Mennon Williams refused to sign extradition papers, and Alabama finally stopped its efforts to have Patterson returned. However, that same year, Patterson killed a man in Michigan and, in 1951, was sentenced to fifteen to twenty years in prison. When he entered the prison, he was found to have lung cancer. The cancer escalated quickly, and Haywood Patterson died in prison in 1952.

Not until May of 1950, just over nineteen years from his arrest, was Andy Wright, the remaining Scottsboro Boy, released from prison. Chalmers had gotten him a job as a hospital orderly in Albany, New York, and Wright swiftly left Alabama. The Scottsboro cases seemed at last to come to an end. But all was not yet over.

In 1969, Dan T. Carter, a scholar and historian, published his definitive book, *Scottsboro: A Tragedy of the American South* (Louisiana State University Press). Earlier, in 1968, he had written an article on the same subject for *American Heritage*. The book was reviewed favorably in over 150 journals, magazines, and newspapers and caught the attention of Tomorrow Entertainment, Inc., which decided that the material would make a good television "docudrama." With a script by screenwriter John McGreevey, "Judge Horton and the Scottsboro Boys" was produced and sold to NBC and broadcast in 1976.

In the first edition of his book, Carter had ended by noting that, according to Scottsboro newspaper editor Fred Bucheit, both Ruby Bates and Victoria Price had died in 1961.[6] But, as Carter and NBC were soon to discover, this was not the case. Soon after the airing of the television show, NBC was notified that both women were alive and well and intended to sue NBC for libel and invasion of privacy.

Victoria Price was living in a small town in Tennessee under the name of Katherine Queen Victory Street. She had married for the fourth time in the 1950s, a sharecropper named Walter Dean Street. Ruby Bates had left the South in 1940 and moved to Washington State, where, in 1942, she had married Elmer Schut, a carpenter. She was then known as Lucille Schut and had returned to the South in the early 1960s when her husband, who was ill, entered a Veterans' Administration hospital. She herself was in poor health in 1976, when the television program aired, and died on Wednesday, October 27, 1976, before the lawsuit was settled.

On July 6, 1977, Judge Charles Neese of the U.S. District Court for the Eastern District of Tennessee, where Victoria Price Street now lived, convened *Victoria Price Street v. The National Broadcasting Company*. Victoria Street was represented by two local lawyers, Raymond Fraley and Don Wyatt. They contended that not only did the television program invade her privacy, but that it was libelous because of false information, and that this was the fault of NBC.

Lasting throughout most of the month of July, the

trial dredged up all the old questions that had emerged in 1931 and in the trials thereafter. Had Victoria Price lied about the assault? Trial transcripts from the 1930s resurfaced and were read once again, and once again the injustice rose to confront the public. When it was all over, Judge Neese dismissed the suit; Price's lawyers had not shown that NBC was at fault, nor had they shown that NBC had exhibited malice toward Price in airing the program. As Dan Carter noted, "For the first time in all the trials in which she testified, Victoria Price Street would not have the vindication of a favorable jury verdict."[7] Times had changed.

Times also proved favorable to Clarence Norris. In October of 1976, after petitioning Alabama from New York, where he lived, Norris received a letter from the state attorney, Bill Baxley. After reviewing Norris's case, Baxley wrote the Pardons and Paroles Board of Alabama:

> I again vigorously appeal to this board to review all the evidence in this case and swiftly grant to Clarence Norris a full and complete pardon. Mr. Norris will continue to live a nightmare until this board removes from him the unjust stigma of conviction for a crime which the overwhelming evidence clearly shows he did not commit.[8]

On November 29, 1976, the Alabama Board of Pardons and Paroles granted Clarence Norris a complete pardon. Justice had been done at last—forty-five years late.

AFTERWORD

More than sixty years have passed since that afternoon in Paint Rock, Alabama, when nine young men and boys were pulled from a slow freight train and soon became known as the Scottsboro Boys. Even today there are those who question how such an injustice could have been done to the "nine captured, caged, tortured, broken, battered and destroyed human beings."[1]

For a great many of those born since the 1960s, the issues of racial justice and equality are, too often, taken for granted. The 1960s with its civil rights movement seemed to mark the culmination of a struggle that began when the United Stated was first settled. For many, it is easy to forget that in Alabama in 1931 the battle had barely begun.

Both the times and the color of their skin worked against the Scottsboro Boys. It was their deep misfortune to be riding a train through a state in which Jim Crow laws were an institution. It was their misfortune that it was during the Great Depression and two white girls saw an opportunity to escape arrest for vagrancy and, perhaps, gain notoriety by accusing the nine of assault. And it was their misfortune that so many saw their plight as a means of promoting an ideology or professional career. Unjustly accused, tugged back and forth by arguments that didn't mean anything to them, nine men's lives were destroyed.

Yet some good did result. In both *Powell v. Alabama* and *Norris v. Alabama*, the United States Supreme Court reaffirmed the basic legal rights of all citizens, and, in particular, of African Americans. Both the good and the bad of Scottsboro should be remembered. Judge James E. Horton, speaking on behalf of the Scottsboro Boys in 1933, realized that, in a number of ways, these cases affected the very foundation of our society:

> Social order is based on law, and its perpetuity on its fair and impartial administration. Deliberate injustice is more fatal to the one who imposes than to the one on whom it is imposed. The victim may die quickly and his suffering cease, but the teachings of Christianity and the uniform lessons of all history illustrate without exception that its perpetrators not only pay the penalty themselves, but their children through endless generations.[2]

NOTES

Chapter 1: Hard Times A-Coming

1. Gilbert Osofsky, *The Burden of Race: A Documentary History of Negro-White Relations in America* (New York: Harper & Row, 1967), pp. 330–31.
2. Sir Paul Harvey, ed., *The Chronological History of the Negro in America* (London: Oxford University Press, 1962), p. 502.
3. Mark Naison, *Communists in Harlem During the Depression* (Urbana, Ill.: University of Illinois Press, 1983), p. 36.

Chapter 2: Paint Rock, Alabama

1. Haywood Patterson and Earl Conrad, *Scottsboro Boy* (Garden City, N.Y.: Doubleday & Co., 1950), p. 28.
2. Ibid., p. 3.
3. Clarence Norris and Sybil Washington, *The Last of the Scottsboro Boys* (New York: G. P. Putnam's Sons, 1979), p. 19.
4. Patterson and Conrad, p. 4.
5. Dan T. Carter, *Scottsboro: A Tragedy of the American South* (Baton Rouge, La.: Louisiana State University Press, 1979), p. 5.
6. Norris and Washington, p. 21.
7. Ibid.

8. Ibid.
9. Ibid., p. 22.

Chapter 3: "A Fair and Lawful Trial"

1. As quoted in Carter, p. 18.
2. Norris and Washington, p. 22.
3. Ibid., p. 23.
4. *Weems v. Alabama*, as quoted in Carter, p. 27.
5. Carter, pp. 48–50.
6. Ibid., p. 32.
7. *Moore v. Dempsey*, as quoted in Carter, p. 13.
8. Patterson and Conrad, p. 13.
9. Norris and Washington, p. 24.
10. Patterson and Conrad, p. 249.

Chapter 4: "Let Those Pore Boys Get Free"

1. Carter, p. 50.
2. Ibid., pp. 52–53.
3. Norris and Washington, p. 26.
4. Carter, p. 57.
5. Norris and Washington, p. 49.
6. Ibid., p. 59.
7. Ibid., p. 102.

Chapter 5: *Powell v. Alabama*

1. Carter, p. 155.
2. Norris and Washington, p. 61.
3. Carter, p. 157.
4. Leonard Levy et al., eds., *Encyclopedia of the American Constitution* (New York: Macmillan, 1986), vol. 3, p. 1433.
5. Patterson and Conrad, pp. 253, 256.
6. Ibid., p. 34.
7. Carter, p. 165.

8. Norris and Washington, p. 49.
9. Patterson and Conrad, pp. 258–59.
10. Carter, p. 187.

Chapter 6: Another "Fair Trial"

1. Carter, p. 182.
2. Norris and Washington, p. 63.
3. Carter, p. 184.
4. Norris and Washington, p. 64
5. Carter, pp. 202–3.
6. Ibid., p. 204.
7. Patterson and Conrad, p. 40.
8. Carter, p. 205.
9. Ibid., p. 210.
10. Ibid., p. 215.
11. Patterson and Conrad, p. 41.
12. Ibid.
13. Carter, p. 235.
14. *New York Times*, April 9, 1933, p. 1.
15. Ibid.
16. Patterson and Conrad, p. 44.
17. Norris and Washington, p. 66.
18. Ibid., pp. 76–77.
19. Patterson and Conrad, p. 48.

Chapter 7: Callahan's Court

1. Norris and Washington, p. 79.
2. Patterson and Conrad, p. 49.
3. Carter, p. 281.
4. Ibid., p. 284.
5. Ibid.
6. Ibid., p. 291.
7. Patterson and Conrad, p. 279.
8. Carter, p. 299.
9. Ibid.

10. Norris and Washington, p. 80.
11. Carter, p. 300.
12. Patterson and Conrad, p. 50.
13. Norris and Washington, p. 80.
14. Carter, p. 302.
15. *New York Times*, May 26, 1934, p. 10.
16. Carter, p. 308.
17. Norris and Washington, p. 145.

Chapter 8: *Norris v. Alabama*

1. Carter, pp. 313–14.
2. Ibid., p. 314.
3. *New York Times*, February 19, 1935, p. 42.
4. Carter, p. 324.
5. Patterson and Conrad, p. 281.
6. Ibid., p. 282.
7. Ibid., pp. 282–83.
8. *New York Times*, April 2, 1935, p. 15.
9. Patterson and Conrad, p. 284.
10. Norris and Washington, p. 147.

Chapter 9: Back to Decatur

1. Carter, pp. 338–39.
2. Ibid.
3. Patterson and Conrad, p. 61.
4. Carter, pp. 341–42.
5. Patterson and Conrad, p. 62.
6. Carter, p. 345.
7. *New York Times*, January 23, 1936, p. 1.
8. Ibid., p. 346.
9. Patterson and Conrad, p. 62.
10. Norris and Washington, p. 162.
11. Ibid., p. 163.
12. Ibid., p. 166.

13. Carter, p. 352.
14. Ibid., p. 364.

Chapter 10: Final Trials and Tribulations

1. Norris and Washington, p. 169.
2. *New York Times*, July 15, 1937, p. 11.
3. Ibid., July 24, 1937, p. 30.
4. Ibid., July 25, 1937, p. 1.
5. Norris and Washington, p. 171.
6. Ibid.
7. Ibid.
8. Patterson and Conrad, p. 68.
9. Carter, p. 377.
10. Ibid., p. 378.
11. Patterson and Conrad, p. 291.
12. Carter, p. 389.
13. Norris and Washington, p. 174.
14. Patterson and Conrad, p. 69.

Chapter 11: The Aftermath

1. Carter, p. 385.
2. Ibid., p. 402.
3. The Montgomery *Advertiser*, February 16, 1940.
4. Carter, pp. 407–8.
5. Ibid., p. 412.
6. Ibid., p. 415.
7. Ibid., p. 459.
8. Norris and Washington, pp. 280–81.

Afterword

1. Carter, p. 462.
2. Patterson and Conrad, pp. 260–61.

BIBLIOGRAPHY

Carmen, Harry J., et al. *A History of the American People.* Vol. 2: *Since 1865.* 3rd ed. New York: Alfred A. Knopf, 1967.

Carter, Dan T. *Scottsboro: A Tragedy of the American South.* Revised ed. Baton Rogue, La.: Louisiana State University Press, 1979.

Chalmers, Allan Knight. *They Shall Be Free.* Garden City, N.Y.: Doubleday & Co., 1951.

Hays, Arthur Garfield. *Trial by Prejudice.* New York: Covici, Friede, 1933.

Levy, Leonard, et al., eds. *Encyclopedia of the American Constitution.* Vol. 3. New York: Macmillan, 1986.

Naison, Mark. *Communists in Harlem During the Depression.* Urbana, Ill.: University of Illinois Press, 1983.

Norris, Clarence, and Sybil D. Washington. *The Last of the Scottsboro Boys.* New York: G. P. Putnam's Sons, 1979.

Patterson, Haywood, and Earl Conrad. *Scottsboro Boy.* Garden City, N.Y.: Doubleday & Co., 1950.

Phillips, Cabell. *The New York Times Chronicle of American Life From the Crash to the Blitz, 1929–1939.* New York: Macmillan, 1969.

INDEX

Agriculture, 7–8
Alabama National Guard, 19,
    25, 29, 55, 59, 63
Alabama Pardons and Paroles
    Board, 93, 98, 99–100,
    103
Alabama Supreme Court,
    43–46, 47, 69–70, 74, 75,
    87, 92, 93
Alexander, Frank, 37
American Civil Liberties Union
    (ACLU), 27, 39, 79
American Scottsboro
    Committee, 70, 72, 79
Atmore Prison Farm, 94,
    99–100

Bailey, H. G., 25–26, 27, 29,
    31, 90
Bates, Emma, 89
Bates, Ruby, 16–17, 19, 20, 21,
    56–57, 81, 102
  absent from Patterson's third
    trial, 65–66
  background and character of,
    39, 53, 58
  letter written by, 50–51

testimony of, 26, 27–28, 53,
    58–59, 68
Baxley, Bill, 103
Beals, Carleton, 83
Beddow, Roderick, 38, 40
Birmingham *Age Herald*, 95
Birmingham *News*, 43
Birmingham *Post*, 68–69
Blalock, Edgar, 85, 86, 87, 91,
    100
Bridges, R. R., 26, 27, 56–57,
    65, 84, 88
Briggs, Cyril, 12
Brodsky, Joseph R., 35, 38–39,
    44, 47, 54, 70
Bryan, William Jennings, 41
Bucheit, Fred, 102
Burden of Race, The (Osofsky),
    5

Callahan, William Washington,
    63–70, 75, 80–84, 87–91
Carmichael, A. A., 87
Carter, Dan T., 34, 56, 57, 87,
    101–2, 103
Chalmers, Allan, 92–94, 95,
    96, 98, 99, 100, 101

Chalmers, George, 82, 84
Chamlee, George W., Sr., 36,
  38–39, 43, 44–45, 47, 51,
  54, 69, 70, 73
Chappell, James Edward, 95
Chattanooga Bar Association,
  51
Chattanooga Daily Times,
  28
Chattanooga Ministers'
  Alliance, 34, 35, 36
Chattanooga News, 86
Christian Century, 67
Commission on Interracial
  Cooperation, 39
Communist, The, 10
"Communist International
  Resolution on the Negro
  Question in U.S., The," 10
Communist Party of America,
  3–4, 9–12, 52
  black membership in, 9,
  10–12, 33
  Depression and, 9–11
  Scottsboro Boys and, 33–34,
  76
  see also International Labor
  Defense
Constitution, U.S., 38, 46, 48,
  54, 64, 74, 76

Daily Worker, 34, 37
Darrow, Clarence, 40–41, 52
Davis, Benjamin, 72
Decatur Daily, 67
Depression, Great, 4, 7–11, 13,
  104
  collapse of agricultural
  industry and, 7–8
  Communist Party's
  popularity in, 9–11

crash of 1929 and, 5–6
  racial disparities intensified
  by, 7
Du Bois, W. E. B., 7

Federal Bureau of Investigation
  (FBI), 101
Fort, Beddow and Ray, 38
Fosdick, Harry Emerson, 58
Fourteenth Amendment, 38,
  48, 54, 74, 76
Fraenkel, Osmond K., 69, 73,
  80
Fraley, Raymond, 102

Gilley, Orville, 20–21, 65, 82
Golden, Obie, 82
Graves, Bibb, 77–78, 81,
  92–95, 96
Great Southern Railroad,
  13–14
  Scottsboro Boys incident and,
  14–17
Green, John, 67

Hackworth, John A., 80
Hall, Grover, 94, 96, 98
Harding, John Vreeland, 65
Harlem Unemployment
  Council, 11
Harten, Thomas C., 97
Hawkins, Alfred E., 22, 23, 25,
  26, 27, 29, 30, 31, 37–38,
  40, 44, 45, 49–50, 53
Hays, Arthur, 41
Heflin, Thomas J., 98–99
Hitler, Adolf, 4, 96
Hoboes, 8, 14
Horton, James Edwin, Jr.,
  54–61, 63, 64, 105

Hughes, Charles Evans, 75–76

Hutson, Melvin, 82–83, 84

Interdenominational Ministers' Alliance, 24

International Labor Defense (ILD), 11–12, 31–32, 34, 35–43

bribery affair and, 70–71

defense coalition formed by, 79

Leibowitz's conflict with, 71–73, 76–77

NAACP's conflict with, 34, 35–37, 40, 41

Scottsboro Boys' appeals and, 38–39, 43–47, 49–50, 51, 52–61, 64–68, 69, 70–74, 76, 79

Isolationism, 7

Jackson County Sentinel, 20, 22, 38, 39

Jim Crow laws, 6, 104

Johnston, Forney, 92, 94

"Judge Horton and the Scottsboro Boys," 101–3

Jury lists, exclusion of Negroes from, 44, 45, 54, 64–65, 69–70, 73, 74–76, 77, 81

Kilby Prison, 31, 35, 49, 68, 82, 94, 99

Knight, Thomas G., Jr., 45, 47, 53–54, 55–56, 57, 58, 59, 61, 64, 69–70, 73, 74, 75, 81, 84, 85, 86–87, 90

Knight, Thomas G., Sr., 45

Kone, Sol, 71

Ku Klux Klan, 34

Latham, Charlie, 16, 17, 20

Lawson, Thomas, 88, 90, 91

League for Industrial Democracy (LID), 79

Leibowitz, Samuel, 52–59, 64–68, 69, 74, 76–78, 82, 84, 86–92, 97

Alabamians' resentment of, 79–80

ILD's conflict with, 71–73, 76–77

Lynch, Marvin, 27, 57

McGreevey, John, 101

Methodist Federation for Social Service, 79

Miller, Ben, 19, 31, 33

Milton, George Fort, 86

Montgomery, Olen, 14, 18, 40, 45, 48

first trial of, 26, 30, 31

freeing of, 91–92, 96–98

Montgomery Advertiser, 77

Moody, J. E., 64

Moody, Milo C., 23–24, 25–26, 28, 29, 38

Morris, Luther, 28

National Association for the Advancement of Colored People (NAACP), 7, 12

ILD's conflict with, 34, 35–37, 40, 41

Scottsboro Boys and, 34–35, 36–38, 40–42, 43, 79, 86, 98

National Urban League, 12

NBC, 101–3
Neese, Charles, 102, 103
New York Interdenominational
    Association of Preachers,
    72
New York Times, 37, 44, 48,
    78, 83
Norris, Clarence, 14, 18, 19,
    45, 49, 53, 54, 63, 78, 82,
    85, 86, 87, 94, 99
  on defense lawyers, 24, 35
  failed pardon deal for, 92–95,
    96
  first trial of, 26–30, 31
  and freeing of other
    Scottsboro Boys, 91–92
  ILD-Leibowitz conflict and,
    71, 72, 73
  ILD-NAACP rivalry and, 37,
    40, 41
  pardon of, 103
  parole and flight of, 100
  second trial of, 67–70
  Supreme Court appeal of, 73,
    74–77, 105
  third trial of, 84, 87, 88–89,
    92, 93
Norris v. Alabama, 73, 74–77,
    105

"Okies," 8
Osofsky, Gilbert, 5

Patterson, Haywood, 18, 21,
    28, 40, 45, 48, 62, 68, 72,
    73, 76, 94, 99
  escape of, 100–101
  failed pardon deal for, 92–95,
    96
  first trial of, 26, 29–30, 31
    fourth trial of, 81–84, 87, 92,
    93
  incident on train as described
    by, 14–15, 16
  second trial of, 54–61
  third trial of, 63–67, 68–70,
    73–74
Patterson, Janie, 37
Patterson, William L., 52–53,
    65
Pearlman, Miron, 50–51
Pearson, J. T., 70, 71
Pickens, William, 37
Pollak, Walter, 46–47, 73–74
Powell, Ozie, 14, 40, 41, 45,
    93, 94, 96, 99, 100
  first trial of, 26, 30, 31
  and incident on road to
    Birmingham jail, 85–86,
    87, 91
  second trial of, 90–91
Powell v. Alabama, 46–49,
    105
Price, Victoria, 16–17, 19,
    20–21, 56–57, 58, 83
  background and character of,
    26–27, 39, 53, 56, 58, 78,
    82, 89
  bribery of, 70–71
  libel suit of, 102–3
  testimony of, 26, 27, 28, 53,
    55–56, 65, 66, 68, 81–82,
    88

Richmond *Times-Dispatch*, 92
Roberson, Willie, 14, 18, 40,
    45
  first trial of, 26, 30, 31
  freeing of, 91–92, 96–97
Roddy, Stephen, 24, 25–27, 28,

29–30, 31, 34–36, 38,
44–45, 48, 51

Sandlin, J. Street, 85, 86
Schriftman, Samuel, 70–71
Schwab, Irving, 53
*Scottsboro: A Tragedy of the
American South* (Carter),
56, 101–2
Scottsboro Boys:
and appeals to Alabama
Supreme Court, 43–46, 47,
69–70, 74, 75, 87, 92,
93
and appeals to U.S. Supreme
Court, 44, 46–49, 69, 70,
72, 73–77, 92, 105
arrest of, 16–17
change of venue motions
and, 25, 50, 53, 64, 80
Communist Party and,
33–34, 76; *see also*
International Labor
Defense
on death row in Kilby Prison,
49
events leading to arrest of,
14–16
failed pardon deal for, 92–95,
96
first trials of, 22, 23–31
freeing of, 91–101
held in Scottsboro jail, 17–
22
identified in lineup, 19
incident on road to
Birmingham jail and,
85–86, 87, 89
indicted by grand juries, 22,
78

motions for new trials for,
38–39
NAACP and, 34–35, 36–38,
40–42, 43, 79, 86, 98
public support for, 33, 34,
37, 46, 68, 96
retrials of, 49–50, 52–70,
79–84, 87, 88–91
sentenced to death, 30, 31
television "docudrama"
about, 101–3
tried separately, 26
see also Montgomery, Olen;
Norris, Clarence;
Patterson, Haywood;
Powell, Ozie; Roberson,
Willie; Weems, Charlie;
Williams, Eugene; Wright,
Andy; Wright, Roy
Scottsboro Defense Committee
(SDC), 79–80, 84, 87,
92–95, 97, 98, 100
Scottsboro *Progressive Age*, 20,
22
Segregation, 6
Shapiro, Morris, 93, 94
Sixth Amendment, 48
Starnes, Joseph, 25
Stephens, P. A., 36
Stock market crash (1929), 5–6
Strauder v. West Virginia, 54
Supreme Court, U.S., 30, 54,
80, 81
Scottsboro Boys' appeals in,
44, 46–49, 69, 70, 72,
73–77, 92, 105
Sutherland, George, 47–48

Thomas, Norman, 86
Traub, Allan, 35

Victoria Price Street v. The National Broadcasting Company, 102–3

Wallace, Sol, 89
Wann, M. L., 16, 19, 25
Watson, Richard S., 89
Watts, Clarence, 82, 83, 84, 88, 89
Weems, Charlie, 14, 18, 40, 41, 42, 45, 68, 87, 99, 100
  failed pardon deal for, 92–95, 96
  first trial of, 26–30, 31
  second trial of, 89–90, 92, 93
White, Walter, 34–35, 36, 38, 40, 41, 42
Williams, Eugene, 14, 18, 21, 40, 45–46, 78

first trial of, 26, 30, 31, 45
freeing of, 91–92, 96–97
Williams, G. Mennon, 101
Wright, Andy, 14, 17–18, 21, 40, 45, 48, 99, 100, 101
  failed pardon deal for, 92–95, 96
  first trial of, 26, 30, 31
  second trial of, 89, 92, 93
Wright, Charlie, 87
Wright, Roy, 14, 17–18, 21–22, 40, 78, 85, 86
  first trial of, 26, 30–31, 44
  freeing of, 91–92, 96–98
  suicide of, 98
Wright, Wade, 59
Wyatt, Don, 102